FACTASTIC
BOOK OF
COMPARISONS

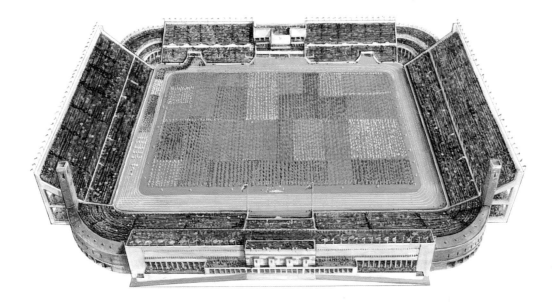

FACTASTIC
BOOK OF
COMPARISONS

RUSSELL ASH

DK

DORLING KINDERSLEY
LONDON • NEW YORK • DELHI • SYDNEY

DK

A DORLING KINDERSLEY BOOK
www.dk.com

Art Editors Dominic Zwemmer,
Dorian Spencer Davies, Joanna Pocock
Project Editors Patrick Newman, Linda Sonntag
Editor Tim Hetherington
Senior Art Editor Dorian Spencer Davies
Senior Managing Art Editor Peter Bailey
Managing Editor Sarah Phillips
DTP Designer Karen Nettelfield
Production Charlotte Traill

Produced for Dorling Kindersley by
PAGE*One*, Cairn House,
Elgiva Lane, Chesham, Bucks, HP5 2JD

Part One first published as *Incredible Comparisons* in 1996;
Part Two first published as *The World in One Day* in 1997;
by Dorling Kindersley Limited,
9 Henrietta Street, London WC2E 8PS

A CIP catalogue record for this book is available
from the British Library

ISBN 0 7513-6208-5

Reproduced in Great Britain by Dot Gradations Limited, Essex
Printed and bound in Italy by L.E.G.O., Vicenza

The day featured throughout section two of this book is not any
particular one, but a typical day in the late 1990s. Of course, there
may be certain days when fewer babies are born, or more rice is
harvested, for example, but such figures, like all those that follow,
are based on daily averages that have been calculated from
authoritative statistics for longer periods.

CONTENTS

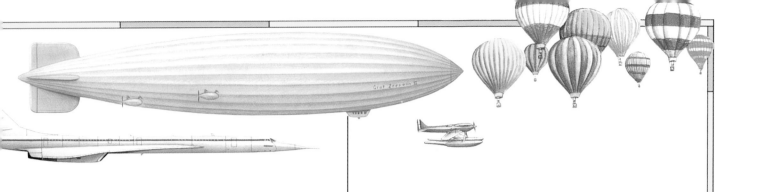

PART TWO
THE WORLD IN ONE DAY

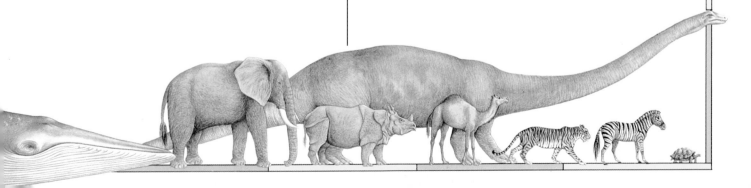

PART ONE
INCREDIBLE
COMPARISONS

HOW TO USE THIS PART

FROM AN EARLY AGE, people with enquiring minds ask such questions as "How big is it?" or "How fast is it?" But even when we learn the answers, it is often hard to grasp what they really mean, especially when dealing with the extraordinary or the unfamiliar. We really want to know how things compare with the commonplace – with the weight of a human, the speed of a car, or the height of a house. *Incredible Comparisons* makes just such comparisons. This is more than a collection of record-breakers, however – there are plenty of averages too. Also, of course, records such as the highest high jump and the tallest building are often broken – but the world's highest mountain will always be just that. Also, while most of the comparisons are between real things, with the illustrations we are able to do things that are impossible in real life. We turn a mountain upside down, lay rail track on Mars, and invite the entire population of the world to move to Bali. By turning the pages, you can join in this exploration of the multitude of comparisons that shape both our world and other worlds beyond.

TURNING THE PAGES

Each time you turn a page you will find a new section on a new topic. Most sections cover two pages, but some open out into four. The section shown here, on *Growth and age*, is two pages.

Averaging out the people

Throughout this section, various things are compared with average size people of different ages. For example, the average two-year-old boy is given to be 84 cm (2 ft 9 in) tall and to weigh 11.8 kg (26 lb).

ABBREVIATIONS USED IN THIS PART					
mm	=	millimetre	°F	=	degrees Fahrenheit
cm	=	centimetre	in	=	inch
m	=	metre	ft	=	foot
km	=	kilometre	oz	=	ounce
kph	=	kilometres per hour	lb	=	pound
g	=	gram	mph	=	miles per hour
kg	=	kilogram	sq	=	square
°C	=	degrees Celsius	%	=	per cent

LARGE NUMBERS		
1,000,000	=	One million (One thousand thousand)
1,000,000,000	=	One billion (One thousand million)
1,000,000,000,000	=	One trillion (One million million)

WEIGHTS AND MEASURES	
1 cm	= 10 mm
1 m	= 100 cm
1 km	= 1,000 m
1 kg	= 1,000 g
1 tonne	= 1,000 kg
1 litre	= 1,000 cubic cm
1 lb	= 16 oz
1 ton	= 2,240 lb
1 ft	= 12 in
1 mile	= 5,280 ft

Talking point
Look out for the voice caption, which appears somewhere in nearly every section – although you are not always able to see who is doing the talking!

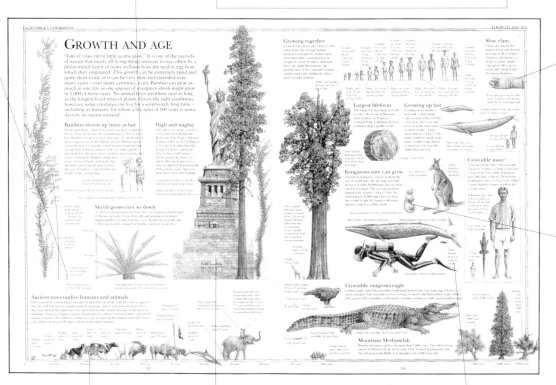

For real
Some of the comparisons are real. This one shows a kind of deep-sea clam that takes 100 years to grow as big as your fingernail.

True size
Some things, such as this baby kangaroo, are shown actual size. A caption tells you when this is the case.

Scales of comparison
In nearly every section there is at least one horizontal or vertical scale, showing such things as the speed, size, and distance of various objects. This way you can make instant, at-a-glance comparisons between the different objects. The horizontal scale here shows how long various trees and animals live.

Moving from page to page
Several familiar objects, such as the Statue of Liberty, shown here, appear on different pages throughout this section. They allow you to make your own comparisons between objects on different pages. Here, the Statue of Liberty stands alongside the world's tallest tree and a single strand of Pacific giant kelp, a kind of seaweed.

Imaginary comparisons
Some of the comparisons are imaginary. For example, this one shows that you would grow up to be as big as an adult blue whale if you were to grow at the same rate as a kangaroo.

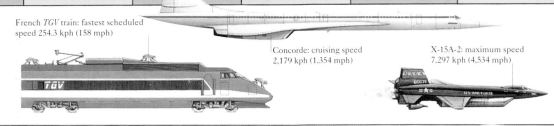

Speed for speed

The French *TGV* train, Concorde, and the X-15A-2 aircraft are among the vehicles that feature regularly. In addition to straightforward speed comparisons, they are used to express long distances in terms of journey times.

French *TGV* train: fastest scheduled speed 254.3 kph (158 mph)

Concorde: cruising speed 2,179 kph (1,354 mph)

X-15A-2: maximum speed 7,297 kph (4,534 mph)

Square by square

Throughout, different surface areas are shown as different size squares. The larger the square, the bigger the surface area. In this example, the squares show the surface areas of different planets. Surface areas are also regularly compared with the area of one or more tennis courts.

Neptune: surface area about 8,024,000,000 sq km (3,098,308,700 sq miles)

Uranus: surface area about 8,209,000,000 sq km (3,169,742,800 sq miles)

Saturn: surface area about 45,644,000,000 sq km (17,624,526,000 sq miles)

Jupiter: surface area about 65,039,000,000 sq km (25,113,522,000 sq miles)

Tennis court: 261 sq m (2,808 sq ft)

By the tubful

Standard bathtub: 80 litres (17.5 gallons)

Volumes of water and other liquids are sometimes given as the number of bathtubs they could fill.

Very large volumes

Very large volumes – such as all the water in the Indian Ocean – are shown as different size cubes. The larger the cube, the bigger the volume.

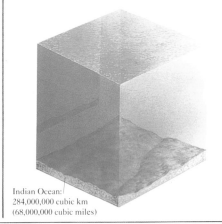

Indian Ocean: 284,000,000 cubic km (68,000,000 cubic miles)

From place to place

New York

Lengths and distances are often compared to the distances between cities. Here the Amazon River is compared to the distance between New York and Berlin.

Berlin

Amazon River

Holding hands all in a line

One way lengths and distances are expressed is in numbers of people holding hands. About 1.2 m (4 ft) is allowed for each person.

Great Wall of China

Height and depth

Buildings and other objects are used throughout to show heights and depths. Some of them are shown here.

Four-storey town house: height 20 m (66 ft)

Empire State Building: height 381 m (1,250 ft)

Eiffel Tower: height 321 m (1,052 ft)

Saturn V rocket: height 111 m (364 ft)

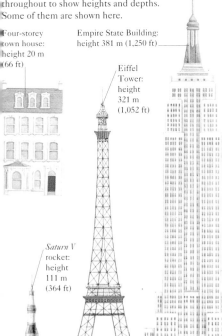

Versatile jumbo

Different facts about Boeing 747 jumbo jets are used to make a variety of comparisons throughout this section.

Cruising speed: 978 kph (608 mph)

Length: 70.4 m (231 ft)

747

BOEING 747

Maximum passenger capacity: 570

Wingspan: 59.6 m (195.5 ft)

Thrust: 101,560 kg (223,898 lb)

Fuel capacity: 217,000 litres (47,734 gallons)

Weighty matters

The weights of different things are compared with the weights of a variety of objects, including a fully grown blue whale and an adult bull African elephant.

A fully grown blue whale might weigh 130 tonnes (128 tons) – or about the same as 26 adult bull African elephants.

An adult bull African elephant weighs about 5 tonnes (5 tons).

ON THE SURFACE

ALL THE LAND on Earth makes up only 29 per cent of the planet's surface – the rest is sea. Three-quarters of all land is forest, desert, and pasture. Most of the rest is farmland, or is under ice. Mountains account for a very small area – towns and cities even less. If you scooped up the largest desert – the Sahara Desert, in northern Africa – and dumped it on the other side of the Atlantic Ocean, it would completely cover the US mainland. Even the tallest skyscrapers would be buried under the massive sand dunes of the Sahara.

Turning forest into farmland

The surface area of Earth totals about 510,000,000 sq km (196,926,400 sq miles). Of that, just 149,200,000 sq km (57,610,626 sq miles) is land. After centuries of clearing trees – for timber, mining, and new farmland – forest still covers the largest part.

Forest	39,000,000 sq km (15,059,077 sq miles)	26 per cent of total land area
Desert	35,300,000 sq km (13,630,396 sq miles)	24 per cent of total land area
Pasture	34,200,000 sq km (13,205,652 sq miles)	23 per cent of total land area
Icecap	15,000,000 sq km (5,791,953 sq miles)	10 per cent of total land area
Cultivated	14,400,000 sq km (5,560,275 sq miles)	10 per cent of total land area
Other	11,300,000 sq km (4,363,271 sq miles)	7 per cent of total land area

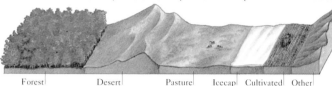

Forest | Desert | Pasture | Icecap | Cultivated | Other

Cross-country by *TGV*

Travelling at its fastest scheduled speed of 254.3 kph (158 mph), the French *TGV*, or High Speed Train, would take under four hours to cover a distance equal to the widest part of its home country. It would take the same train almost 10 times as long, however, to cover a distance equal to the widest part of the largest country in the world, Russia.

France occupies an area of 515,000 sq km (198,857 sq miles). At its widest it measures 974 km (605 miles). The *TGV* could cover this distance in just three hours and 58 minutes.

Vatican not so vast

A state within a state, the tiny Vatican City, in Italy, occupies just 0.44 sq km (0.17 sq miles) – about the same area as 60 soccer pitches, each being 100 m (328 ft) long and 73 m (239.5 ft) wide.

Outsized island

Greenland is the largest island on Earth, covering a total area of 2,175,600 sq km (840,065 sq miles). It is three times as big as Borneo, the second largest island in the world, and nine times as big as Honshu, the main island of Japan. Greenland belongs to Denmark, but if it were a separate country it would actually be the thirteenth largest country in the world.

Honshu, Japan: 230,448 sq km (88,983 sq miles)

Borneo: 744,366 sq km (287,422 sq miles)

Greenland: 2,175,600 sq km (840,065 sq miles)

Covering an area of 2,505,813 sq km (967,570 sq miles), Sudan is the largest country in Africa. At its widest it measures 1,850 km (1,150 miles) – a distance equivalent to a *TGV* journey time of seven hours and 31 minutes.

Australia covers 7,836,848 sq km (3,026,044 sq miles). At its widest it is 3,983 km (2,475 miles) from coast to coast. This is equivalent to a *TGV* journey time of 16 hours and 12 minutes.

I'm nearly there! If I were crossing Russia, however, I wouldn't even have reached the halfway point yet.

The total area of the USA (including Alaska and Hawaii) is 9,529,063 sq km (3,679,459 sq miles). At its widest, the USA is 4,517 km (2,807 miles) from coast to coast – equivalent to a *TGV* journey time of 18 hours and 22 minutes.

Russia is far and away the largest country on Earth, covering 17,075,400 sq km (6,593,328 sq miles). At its widest, Russia is a cross-country journey of 9,650 km (5,996 miles). It would take the *TGV* 39 hours and 14 minutes to cover this distance.

1,000 km (621 miles) | 2,000 km (1,243 miles) | 3,000 km (1,864 miles) | 4,000 km (2,486 miles)

Unbroken border

The longest unbroken frontier in the world – between Canada and the USA – stretches 6,416 km (3,987 miles). This is slightly longer than the Great Wall of China, which totals about 6,400 km (3,977 miles). Allowing some 1.2 m (4 ft) per person, this is equivalent to a line of some 5,300,000 people holding hands.

Fly me to the Moon

The total length of all the world's coastlines is not far short of the average distance between Earth and the Moon. Even at Concorde's supersonic cruising speed of 2,179 kph (1,354 mph) it would take you a week to fly this far.

Concorde

The total length of all the world's coastlines is reckoned to be about 356,000 km (221,214 miles).

The average distance between Earth and the Moon is 384,000 km (238,613 miles).

The border between Canada and the USA is longer than the Great Wall of China.

Each figure represents about 10,000 people.

A decade of deforestation

Clearing tropical rainforest causes loss of valuable plant and animal species, destruction of tribal peoples' ways of life, increased soil erosion, and possibly even global warming. Worldwide, in the 1980s, some 1,541,000 sq km (585,027 sq miles) of rainforest were cleared – about eight per cent of the total area.

Asia and the Pacific: 390,000 sq km (150,591 sq miles) of rainforest lost in the 1980s

Africa: 410,000 sq km (158,313 sq miles) lost in the 1980s

Overall, an area of rainforest larger than Alaska was cleared in the 1980s.

South America and the Caribbean: 741,000 sq km (286,122 sq miles) lost in the 1980s

Asia is biggest

Of the seven continents, the largest, Asia, accounts for almost a third of all the land on Earth.

Europe: 10,000,000 sq km (3,861,302 sq miles) – 7% of the world's land

Oceania: 9,000,000 sq km (3,475,172 sq miles) – 6% of the world's land

Antarctica: 14,000,000 sq km (5,405,823 sq miles) – 9.5% of the world's land

South America: 18,000,000 sq km (6,950,344 sq miles) – 12% of the world's land

North America: 24,000,000 sq km (9,267,125 sq miles) – 16% of the world's land

Africa: 30,000,000 sq km (11,583,906 sq miles) – 20% of the world's land

Asia: 44,000,000 sq km (16,989,728 sq miles) – 29.5% of the world's land

Desert lands that compare to whole countries

About a quarter of all land is desert. Some deserts are semi-arid. Other deserts are extremely arid, with almost no rainfall at all. The Australian Desert is bigger than India, yet it is less than half as big as the enormous Sahara Desert, in northern Africa.

The Kalahari Desert, in southern Africa, covers 520,000 sq km (200,788 sq miles) – an area bigger than France.

Covering 1,040,000 sq km (401,575 sq miles), the Gobi Desert is the largest desert in Asia.

At 1,300,000 sq km (501,969 sq miles), the Arabian Desert is bigger than Peru.

The Australian Desert covers 3,800,000 sq km (1,467,295 sq miles).

The Sahara Desert is the largest desert in the world, covering 9,065,000 sq km (3,500,270 sq miles).

Mountains of desert sand

The world's tallest sand dunes are found in the Sahara. They are big enough to bury big buildings such as the Great Pyramid, in Egypt, and the Eiffel Tower, in Paris.

Some sand dunes in the African Sahara are 465 m (1,526 ft) tall – more than 23 times as tall as a four-storey town house.

Four-storey town house: 20 m (66 ft)

Eiffel Tower: 321 m (1,052 ft)

Great Pyramid: 147 m (481 ft)

An Eiffel lot of ice

The icecap over the South Pole is some 2,800 m (9,186 ft) thick – almost as deep as a stack of nine Eiffel Towers. Incredibly, in some places the Antarctic icecap is 4,780 m (15,682 ft) thick – almost as deep as 15 Eiffel Towers.

Icecap over South Pole: 2,800 m (9,186 ft)

Nine Eiffel Towers: 2,889 m (9,478 ft)

A desert as big as the USA

The Sahara Desert extends across northern Africa. With large expanses receiving little or no rain for years at a time, and an average annual temperature of 27°C (80°F), it is an inhospitable region supporting fewer than 2,000,000 people, mostly on its relatively fertile margins. The Sahara covers an area about the size of mainland USA. The population of the USA is more than 130 times as big, however. Only three countries in the world are bigger than the Sahara Desert: Russia, Canada, and China.

The Sahara Desert could cover the whole of mainland USA.

6,000 km (3,728 miles)   7,000 km (4,350 miles)   8,000 km (4,971 miles)   9,000 km (5,592 miles)   10,000 km (6,214 miles)

INTO THE EARTH

VIEWED FROM SPACE, through the window of an orbiting spacecraft, the Earth appears to be completely smooth, like a multicoloured beachball – yet the surface of our planet is pitted with craters, scored with canyons, and riddled with caves. The deepest hole ever drilled is deeper than the deepest canyon – yet it does not even break through the Earth's crust, which covers the interior of the planet like the skin of a giant apple.

Chasmic canyons

Canyons are very deep, very narrow valleys, with very steep – almost vertical – sides. They are usually found in hot, dry places, where soft or weak rock is rapidly worn through by rivers, but where there is not enough rain to wash away the sides of the river valleys. The great canyons of the USA are the most spectacular of all. At its deepest point, Kings Canyon, in California, is deep enough to swallow a stack of six-and-a-half Empire State Buildings.

Empire State Building, New York: 381 m (1,250 ft) tall

Solid as a rock?

The Earth's crust consists of solid rock, but if you were to break it down into its component elements, nearly half of it would vanish into thin air! This is because almost half of the Earth's crust is made up of just one element – oxygen.

Oxygen: 46.6%

Silicon: 27.7%

Aluminium: 8.1%

Sodium: 2.8%

Iron: 5%

Calcium: 3.6%

Potassium: 2.6%

Magnesium: 2.1%

Hydrogen: 1%

Titanium: 0.5%

The Snake River has gouged out Hells Canyon, in Oregon and Idaho, to a maximum depth of 2,408 m (7,900 ft) – more than three-and-a-half times as deep as the deepest point in the North Sea.

The Grand Canyon, in Arizona, was formed by the Colorado River, and has a maximum depth of 1,600 m (5,249 ft) – equivalent to a stack of 80 four-storey town houses.

The North Sea has a maximum depth of 660 m (2,165 ft). Its average depth, however, is only 94 m (308 ft).

Kings Canyon: maximum depth 2,499 m (8,199 ft)

Colossal craters

Sudbury Crater, in Ontario, Canada, is 140 km (87 miles) wide. It is the largest crater on Earth. There are much bigger craters on the Moon, however – all of them made by meteorites. Bailly Crater, for example, is nearly as wide as the distance from Paris to London.

London

Bailly Crater is the largest crater on the near side of the Moon. On the dark side, however, the Orientale Basin is three times as large.

Caves top canyons

One of the true wonders of the natural world, the mighty Grand Canyon is more than twice as long as Hells Canyon, and nine times as long as Kings Canyon. The combined length of all the caves in the Mammoth Cave system, in Kentucky, in the USA, is even greater, however.

Hello down there! I'm nearly half-way down, but I'm still more than three times as high up as the top of the Empire State Building.

Kings Canyon is in the Sierra Nevada mountains. Unlike Hells Canyon and the Grand Canyon, which were formed solely by river erosion, Kings Canyon was formed by a combination of river erosion and erosion by glaciers.

Four-store town hous 20 m (66 f

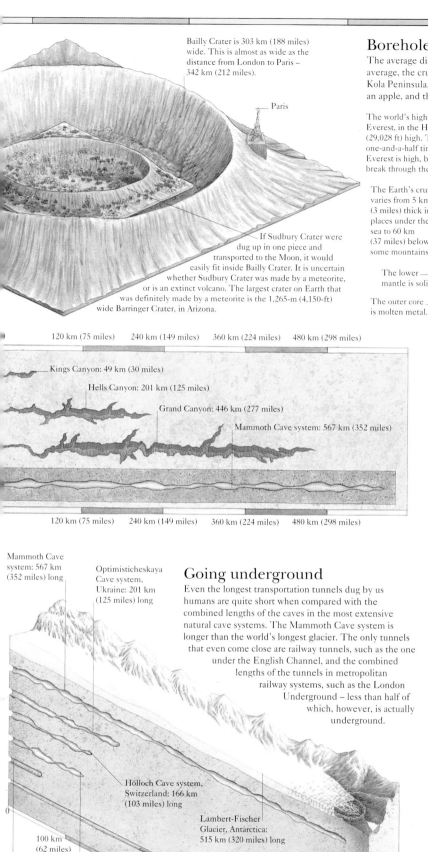

Bailly Crater is 303 km (188 miles) wide. This is almost as wide as the distance from London to Paris – 342 km (212 miles).

Paris

If Sudbury Crater were dug up in one piece and transported to the Moon, it would easily fit inside Bailly Crater. It is uncertain whether Sudbury Crater was made by a meteorite, or is an extinct volcano. The largest crater on Earth that was definitely made by a meteorite is the 1,265-m (4,150-ft) wide Barringer Crater, in Arizona.

120 km (75 miles)   240 km (149 miles)   360 km (224 miles)   480 km (298 miles)

Kings Canyon: 49 km (30 miles)

Hells Canyon: 201 km (125 miles)

Grand Canyon: 446 km (277 miles)

Mammoth Cave system: 567 km (352 miles)

120 km (75 miles)   240 km (149 miles)   360 km (224 miles)   480 km (298 miles)

Going underground

Even the longest transportation tunnels dug by us humans are quite short when compared with the combined lengths of the caves in the most extensive natural cave systems. The Mammoth Cave system is longer than the world's longest glacier. The only tunnels that even come close are railway tunnels, such as the one under the English Channel, and the combined lengths of the tunnels in metropolitan railway systems, such as the London Underground – less than half of which, however, is actually underground.

Mammoth Cave system: 567 km (352 miles) long

Optimisticheskaya Cave system, Ukraine: 201 km (125 miles) long

Hölloch Cave system, Switzerland: 166 km (103 miles) long

Lambert-Fischer Glacier, Antarctica: 515 km (320 miles) long

London Underground railway system: 408 km (254 miles) long

0

100 km (62 miles)

200 km (124 miles)

300 km (186 miles)

400 km (249 miles)

500 km (311 miles)

English Channel railway tunnel from the UK to France: 50 km (31 miles) long

Jewel Cave system, South Dakota, USA: 174 km (108 miles) long

Borehole barely pricks the skin

The average distance to the centre of the Earth is 6,378 km (3,963 miles). On average, the crust is 24 km (15 miles) thick. The deepest hole ever drilled – at Kola Peninsula, in Russia – is about 12 km (7.5 miles) deep. If the Earth were an apple, and the crust its skin, this hole would not even pierce the skin.

The world's highest mountain, Mt Everest, in the Himalayas, is 8,848 m (29,028 ft) high. The Kola borehole is one-and-a-half times as deep as Mt Everest is high, but does not even break through the Earth's crust.

The Earth's crust varies from 5 km (3 miles) thick in places under the sea to 60 km (37 miles) below some mountains.

The lower mantle is solid.

The outer core is molten metal.

Upper mantle: mostly solid, with a liquid layer

The inner core is a solid ball of intensely hot iron under extreme pressure.

0

3,000 m (9,843 ft)

6,000 m (19,685 ft)

9,000 m (29,528 ft)

12,000 m (39,370 ft)

15,000 m (49,213 ft)

Western Deep Levels gold mine, South Africa: 3,777 m (12,392 ft)

Oil boreholes rarely extend deeper than 9,100 m (29,856 ft).

In 1970, a geological survey team began to bore a hole at the Kola Peninsula. By April 1992 it was 12,262 m (40,230 ft) deep.

How low can you get?

Some places on Earth lie below sea level, the average level of the surface of the oceans. Known as depressions, they usually result from deformations or folds in the Earth's crust.

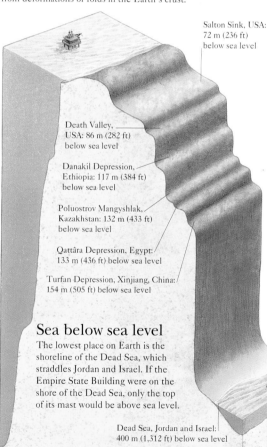

Salton Sink, USA: 72 m (236 ft) below sea level

Death Valley, USA: 86 m (282 ft) below sea level

Danakil Depression, Ethiopia: 117 m (384 ft) below sea level

Poluostrov Mangyshlak, Kazakhstan: 132 m (433 ft) below sea level

Qattâra Depression, Egypt: 133 m (436 ft) below sea level

Turfan Depression, Xinjiang, China: 154 m (505 ft) below sea level

Sea below sea level

The lowest place on Earth is the shoreline of the Dead Sea, which straddles Jordan and Israel. If the Empire State Building were on the shore of the Dead Sea, only the top of its mast would be above sea level.

Dead Sea, Jordan and Israel: 400 m (1,312 ft) below sea level

Jupiter: average distance from the Sun
778,330,000 km (483,645,060 miles)

Saturn: average distance from the Sun
1,426,980,000 km (886,708,500 miles)

750,000,000 km
(466,041,130 miles)

1,000,000,000 km
(621,388,180 miles)

1,500,000,000 km
(932,082,270 miles)

2,000,000,000 km
(1,242,776,300 miles)

500°C
(932°F)

Venus is a searing
464°C (867°F).

Temperatures on
Mercury range from
a scorching 430°C
(806°F) to –200°C
(–328°F).

400°C
(752°F)

300°C
(572°F)

200°C
(392°F)

Temperatures on
Earth range from
60°C (140°F) to
–89°C (–128°F).

100°C
(212°F)

0°C
(32°F)

–100°C
(–148°F)

–200°C
(–328°F)

–300°C
(–508°F)

Temperatures on
Mars range from
27°C (81°F) to
–140°C (–220°F).

Jupiter is
about
–145°C
(–229°F).

Saturn is
about
–180°C
(–292°F).

Neptune
is about
–220°C
(–364°F).

Uranus is about
–223°C (–369°F).

Pluto is about
–230°C (–382°F).

Jupiter is a drag for jumpers

On Jupiter, where
gravity is 2.6 times that
on Earth, a common
flea could jump up to
13 cm (5 in).

The men's long jump record on
Jupiter would be 3.4 m (11 ft).

The 1.5-mm (0.06-in) common flea can jump up to 220
times its body size lengthways. This is equivalent to a 1.65-m
(5-ft 5-in) woman jumping 363 m (1,191 ft) in the long jump. On the
Moon, both fleas and humans could jump six times as far as they can on
Earth. But even fleas would struggle against the dragging gravity of Jupiter.

0   8 m (26 ft)   16 m (52 ft)   24 m (79 ft)   32 m (105 ft)   40 m (131 ft)   48 m (157 ft)

On Earth, a common flea can jump up to 33 cm (13 in).

The world long jump record for men is 8.95 m (29 ft 4.5 in).

0   8 m (26 ft)   16 m (52 ft)   24 m (79 ft)   32 m (105 ft)   40 m (131 ft)   48 m (157 ft)

On the Moon, a common flea could jump up to 2 m (6.5 ft).

On the Moon, the men's long jump
record would be 53.7 m (176 ft).

0   8 m (26 ft)   16 m (52 ft)   24 m (79 ft)   32 m (105 ft)   40 m (131 ft)   48 m (157 ft)

Frying and freezing

Life can exist on Earth because of our
world's moderate temperatures. No
other planet in the Solar System has
such favourable conditions. Some, like
Pluto, are icy rocks; others, like Venus,
are fiery furnaces. Mercury is both.

Grains of sunshine the size of France

Seen in close-up through a special solar telescope, the surface of the Sun looks
grainy. The grains are actually gigantic columns of gas, each about 1,000 km
(621 miles) wide – about as big as France. Each column of gas rises and falls at
regular five-minute intervals. (To protect your eyes from damage, never look
directly at the Sun – especially not with an ordinary telescope or binoculars.)

The surface of the
Sun is covered with
huge columns of gas.

Size is relative

Compared with even the
biggest planet, the Sun is
huge. If the Sun were as
wide as an astronaut is tall,
Jupiter would be the size of
the astronaut's head.
Earth would be the size of
an eye. Compared with
some stars, however, the
Sun is minute. The biggest
known star is Betelgeuse.
If the Sun were the size of
an astronaut, Betelgeuse
would be as wide as a stack
of three Eiffel Towers.

Jupiter:
equatorial
diameter
143,884 km
(89,408 miles)

The Sun:
diameter
1,392,140 km
(865,059 miles)

Eiffel Tower:
321 m (1,052 ft)

Betelgeuse:
diameter
700,000,000 km
(434,971,720 miles)

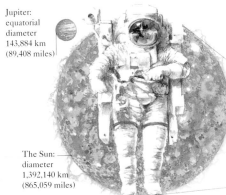

It would take about 3,645,000,000 people holding hands to go
around the 4,374,000-km (2,717,952-mile) equator of the Sun.

Each figure represents about 10,000,000 people.

400,000 km (248,555 miles)   500,000 km (310,694 miles)   600,000 km (372,833 miles)   700,000 km (434,972 miles)

THE SOLAR SYSTEM

AS AN ASTRONAUT on the first voyage to another planet, what should you pack? Let's start with the essentials: don't forget your toothbrush. Actually, you had better pack several – it is a two-year round trip to even the nearest planet to Earth, Mars. What about clothes? Your space suit comes courtesy of the space agency, but you will need casual wear as well. If you are heading away from the Sun, be sure to wrap up warm on the planets beyond Mars, because they are all colder than Antarctica. Venus is warmer, but you can leave your swim-suit behind: you will need a fire-fighter's outfit to survive the searing heat. For the smaller planets, take your trainers. You can look forward to some fun, especially if you were always the last to be picked for the basketball team. On Mars you will be able to jump three times as high as you can on Earth. The bad news is that, under Martian rules, the hoop must be 9 m (30 ft) off the ground.

Sun

Earth: average distance from the Sun 149,600,000 km (92,959,671 miles)

Mars: average distance from the Sun 227,940,000 km (141,639,220 miles)

Mercury: average distance from the Sun 57,910,000 km (35,984,589 miles)

250,000,000 km (155,347,040 miles)

Venus: average distance from the Sun 108,200,000 km (67,234,201 miles)

Pluto keeps its distance

Pluto is the most distant planet. If the Sun were your head, and you whirled Earth around it on the end of a string, you would need a string 40 times as long for Pluto.

Pluto has an equatorial diameter of 2,324 km (1,444 miles). Its one moon, Charon, is 1,270 km (789 miles) wide.

Mercury is 4,878 km (3,031 miles) wide.

Mars has an equatorial diameter of 6,794 km (4,222 miles). It has two tiny moons: Phobos and Deimos.

Venus is 12,104 km (7,521 miles) wide.

The Moon is 3,477 km (2,161 miles) wide.

Earth is 12,756 km (7,926 miles) wide.

Triton

Neptune has an equatorial diameter of 50,538 km (31,404 miles). It has eight moons: the largest, Triton, is 2,705 km (1,681 miles) wide.

Uranus is 51,118 km (31,764 miles) wide at its equator. It has 15 moons: the largest, Titania, is 1,578 km (981 miles) wide.

Titania

Saturn has an equatorial diameter of 120,536 km (74,900 miles). It has 18 moons: the largest, Titan, is 5,150 km (3,200 miles) wide.

Titan

Jupiter is 143,884 km (89,408 miles) wide at its equator. It has 16 moons: the largest, Ganymede, is 5,268 km (3,273 miles) wide.

Ganymede

Ripened by the Sun?

The nine planets orbiting the Sun are as varied in size as the different fruits and vegetables that we eat – the smallest planets are smaller than some of the moons of other planets. If Venus and Earth were plums, Mars would be a gooseberry, Mercury a grape, and Pluto a pea. Neptune and Uranus would be grapefruits, while Saturn and Jupiter would be watermelons. On the same scale, the Sun would be enormous – equivalent to a circular dining table big enough to seat 20 people.

Sizing up the Moon

You can cover the Moon in the sky with a coin held at arm's length. In fact, it is a quarter as wide as Earth, and nearly as wide as Australia.

Earth is 12,756 km (7,926 miles) wide.

The Moon is 3,477 km (2,161 miles) wide.

Australia is 3,983 km (2,475 miles) wide at its widest.

The Sun's diameter is 1,392,140 km (865,059 miles).

Planetary bulges

None of the nine planets is a perfect sphere – they all bulge at their equators, and are flattened at their poles.

Greetings, Earthlings! This space suit felt really heavy back on Earth, but here on the Moon you hardly know you've got it on, and you can leap around all over the place!

On the Moon, an astronaut in a space suit weighs about 22 kg (48 lb).

On Earth, an astronaut in a space suit weighs about 135 kg (298 lb).

Less weighty matters

The less massive the planet or moon, the weaker its gravity. The Moon's gravity is a sixth of that of Earth. On the Moon, therefore, you would weigh a sixth of what you do on Earth, and a single bound would send you soaring.

Holding hands to better understand

The Sun and planets are so large that their sizes are hard to grasp. One way to understand how big they are is to imagine them ringed by people holding hands. Allowing about 1.2 m (4 ft) for each person, the Sun is so enormous that it would take more people than there are in Asia to encircle it. Saturn would take nearly everyone in South America, while Earth would need more people than there are in the whole of Canada. Even Pluto would need about the entire population of Hong Kong.

It would take about 316,000,000 people holding hands to ring the 378,675-km (235,304-mile) equator of Saturn.

It would take about 33,000,000 people holding hands to go around the 40,075-km (24,902-mile) equator of Earth.

It would take about 6,000,000 people holding hands to encircle the 7,300-km (4,536-mile) equator of Pluto.

GOING INTO SPACE

"THREE... TWO... ONE... We have lift-off!" Your seat vibrates, and you start moving upwards, slowly at first, then ever faster. You are on board the world's most powerful vehicle, being thrust into space with the force of 31 jumbo jets. The ride is surprisingly smooth, however – some rollercoasters push you harder into your seat – so you hardly realize you are travelling 10 times faster than a rifle bullet. In orbit, you have a unique view of Earth, floating in the vastness of space. With luck, you might spot a mighty comet the size of France, with a tail as long as five planets. But watch out for meteorites. At orbital velocity, a plum-sized meteorite can do as much damage as a speeding car.

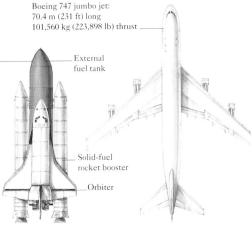

Wind speeds on Neptune, which has an atmosphere of mainly hydrogen, reach 2,000 kph (1,243 mph) – 10 times as fast as the strongest tropical storms on Earth.

| 0 | 1,500 kph (932 mph) | 5,000 kph (3,107 mph) |

The speed of sound through air at ground level on Earth is 1,229 kph (764 mph).

Space is the place for speed

Friction restricts the speed of objects through air. But space is a near vacuum, so probes such as *Helios B* travel many times faster than any object through air. Even the planets move at quite high speeds as they orbit the Sun. The only thing that travels faster through air than through space is sound. The speed of sound in space is zero, because sound cannot travel in a vacuum – space is completely silent.

Cargo space

A space shuttle is a freighter, with a cargo bay big enough to hold a humpback whale – with room to spare for 1,000 or so herring. Alternatively, you could fill it with 250,000 chocolate bars, each weighing 118 g (4 oz).

The cargo bay of a space shuttle is 18.3 m (60 ft) long, and can hold up to 29.5 tonnes (29 tons). A fully grown humpback whale is about 15 m (49 ft) long and weighs about 29 tonnes (28.5 tons).

Standing tall on the launch pad

Launchers at the Kennedy Space Center, in Florida, in the USA, tower over the surrounding marshland. The *Saturn V* rockets, used for the *Apollo* Moon missions in the 1960s and early 1970s, were as tall as a 30-storey building. At lift-off, even a space shuttle is as tall as the Leaning Tower of Pisa, in Italy.

Saturn V rocket (1973): 111 m (364 ft)

Shuttle power

At lift-off, a space shuttle comprises a huge external fuel tank and two solid-fuel rocket boosters as well as the familiar orbiter, and is almost 31 times as powerful as a Boeing 747 jumbo jet. This is because a space shuttle must quickly accelerate to a staggering 28,000 kph (17,400 mph) – nearly four times as fast as the world's fastest ever plane, the X-15A-2 – to get into orbit above the Earth's atmosphere.

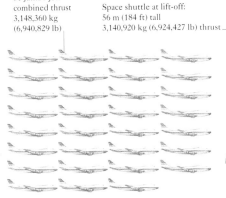

31 jumbo jets: combined thrust 3,148,360 kg (6,940,829 lb)

Space shuttle at lift-off: 56 m (184 ft) tall 3,140,920 kg (6,924,427 lb) thrust

Boeing 747 jumbo jet: 70.4 m (231 ft) long 101,560 kg (223,898 lb) thrust

External fuel tank

Solid-fuel rocket booster

Orbiter

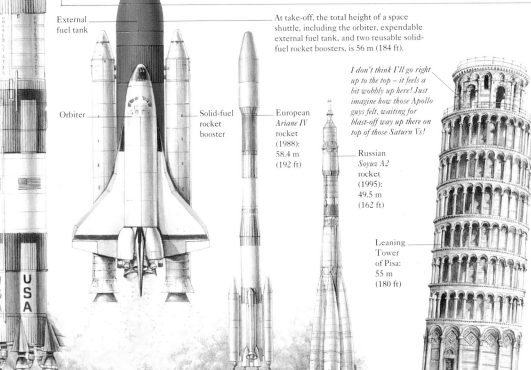

External fuel tank

Orbiter

Solid-fuel rocket booster

At take-off, the total height of a space shuttle, including the orbiter, expendable external fuel tank, and two reusable solid-fuel rocket boosters, is 56 m (184 ft).

European *Ariane IV* rocket (1988): 58.4 m (192 ft)

I don't think I'll go right up to the top – it feels a bit wobbly up here! Just imagine how those Apollo guys felt, waiting for blast-off way up there on top of those Saturn Vs!

Russian *Soyuz A2* rocket (1995): 49.5 m (162 ft)

Leaning Tower of Pisa: 55 m (180 ft)

Compact probe

Space capsules, satellites, and probes are tiny compared with the powerful rocket and shuttle launchers that propel them out of the Earth's atmosphere and into space. The *Giotto* space probe, which flew past Halley's Comet in 1986, was about the same size as a small car.

Giotto space probe: 3.1 m (10 ft)

Collision course

Giotto scientists knew that debris pouring off Halley's Comet would eventually destroy the probe – but not before it had beamed invaluab[le] photographs and data back to Eart[h]

Giotto: 3.1 m (10 ft)

110 m (361 ft)
100 m (328 ft)
90 m (295 ft)
80 m (262 ft)
70 m (230 ft)
60 m (197 ft)
50 m (164 ft)
40 m (131 ft)
30 m (98 ft)
20 m (66 ft)
10 m (33 ft)
0

Pluto: 17,064 kph (10,603 mph)

Neptune: 19,548 kph (12,147 mph)

Uranus: 24,516 kph (15,234 mph)

Mars: 86,868 kph (53,979 mph)

Mercury: 172,404 kph (107,130 mph)

Helios B space probe: 239,987 kph (149,125 mph)

Jupiter: 47,016 kph (29,215 mph)

Earth: 107,244 kph (66,640 mph)

Venus: 126,108 kph (78,362 mph)

10,000 kph (6,214 mph)

Sputnik I: 28,565 kph (17,750 mph)

30,000 kph (18,642 mph)

Saturn: 34,704 kph (21,565 mph)

50,000 kph (31,069 mph)

100,000 kph (62,139 mph)

200,000 kph (124,278 mph)

300,000 kph (186,416 mph)

Apollo 10 capsule re-entering Earth's atmosphere: 39,897 kph (24,792 mph)

Budweiser Rocket car: 1,190 kph (739 mph)

1,000 kph (621 mph)

Concorde: cruising speed 2,179 kph (1,354 mph)

5,000 kph (3,107 mph)

Unmanned rocket sled: 4,972 kph (3,090 mph)

X-15A-2 plane: 7,297 kph (4,534 mph)

10,000 kph (6,214 mph)

30,000 kph (18,642 mph)

50,000 kph (31,069 mph)

Earth's escape velocity, the speed required to escape the clutches of Earth's gravity completely, is 40,250 kph (25,011 mph). It has been exceeded only by unmanned rockets.

Longtailed snowballs

Since the dawn of time, superstitious people all over the world have believed that the sight of a comet streaking across the night sky is a sign of imminent ill fortune. Comets are really just "dirty snowballs" – rough lumps of ice and dust orbiting the Sun – and are actually very small. The most famous, Halley's Comet, is only about 15 km (9 miles) in diameter. Comet tails, by contrast, are huge. The tail of the Great Comet of 1843 was as long as the combined diameters of the three biggest planets, Earth, and Pluto.

Moon dwarfs asteroids

Besides the nine major planets, some 5,000 microplanets, or asteroids, orbit the Sun – mostly between Mars and Jupiter. Their combined mass is less than the mass of the Moon, and some are only a few metres wide. The diameter of the largest, Ceres, is only a quarter the diameter of the Moon.

The diameter of the Moon 3,477 km (2,161 miles).

Jupiter: diameter 143,884 km (89,408 miles)

Saturn: diameter 120,536 km (74,900 miles)

Uranus: diameter 51,118 km (31,764 miles)

Earth: diameter 12,756 km (7,926 miles)

Pluto: diameter 2,324 km (1,444 miles)

The combined diameters of Jupiter, Saturn, Uranus, Earth, and Pluto total 330,618 km (205,442 miles). The tail of the Great Comet of 1843 is about the same length. A comet tail is made up of glowing dust and gas, but these are very thinly spread out. There is more matter in 1 cubic mm (0.0006 cubic in) of air on Earth than in 1 cubic km (0.25 cubic miles) of comet tail.

Ceres: diameter 914 km (568 miles)

France: area 515,000 sq km (198,857 sq miles)

Asteroid impact scenario

If Ceres crashed into Earth it would obliterate an area the size of France, and the dust thrown up would block out the Sun for years to come, causing global climatic change. Such an asteroid collision might have caused the extinction of the dinosaurs. Luckily, Ceres is too far away for us to worry about but another asteroid, Hermes, just missed Earth in 1937, passing only twice as far away as the Moon.

Desert asteroid

If the surface of Ceres were spread out flat it would cover an area slightly greater than that of Saudi Arabia. Since Ceres is a dry rock dotted by meteorite impacts, it might just bear more than a passing resemblance to the Rub al Khali, Saudi Arabia's "Empty Quarter", which is the world's largest continuous area of sand dunes.

Surface area of Ceres: about 2,624,000 sq km (1,013,206 sq miles)

Surface area of Saudi Arabia: 2,149,690 sq km (830,060 sq miles)

Cosmic dustbin

A huge amount of space rock enters the Earth's atmosphere every day. Big pieces fall as meteorites. Sand-sized particles burn up, creating "shooting stars". Specks of dust drift down intact. As much as 40,000 tonnes (39,370 tons) of cosmic dust falls to Earth each year – equal to the weight of more than 300 blue whales.

As much as 40,000 tonnes (39,370 tons) of cosmic dust lands on Earth each year.

The average weight of a blue whale is about 130 tonnes (128 tons).

A stopping distance of six bridges – just in case

A space shuttle glides back to Earth. On landing, it uses parachutes, as well as brakes, to stop. The usual landing site is the world's longest runway, at Edwards Air Force Base, in California. The runway is six times as long as the Golden Gate Bridge, in San Francisco, California – although a shuttle does not need the full length of it.

The Golden Gate Bridge is nearly 2 km (1.25 miles) long.

The runway at Edwards Air Force Base is almost 12 km (7.5 miles) long.

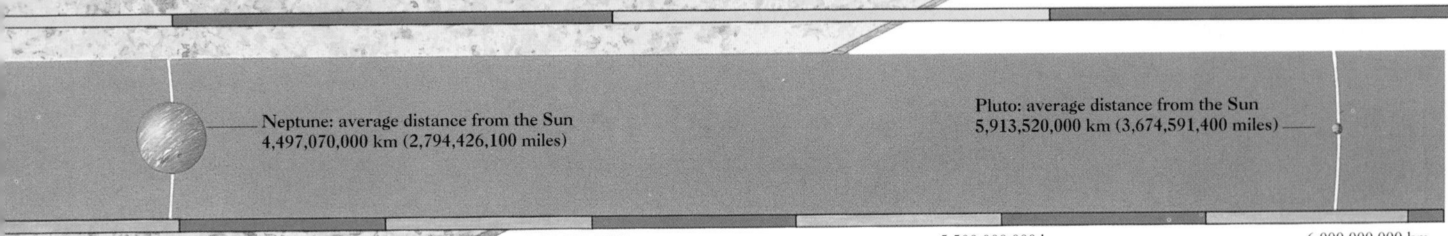

Neptune: average distance from the Sun
4,497,070,000 km (2,794,426,100 miles)

Pluto: average distance from the Sun
5,913,520,000 km (3,674,591,400 miles)

5,000,000,000 km
(3,106,940,900 miles)

5,500,000,000 km
(3,417,634,900 miles)

6,000,000,000 km
(3,728,329,000 miles)

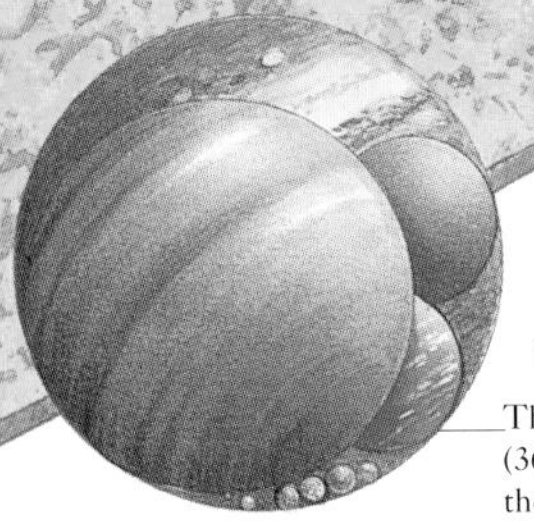

Clay balls

If Jupiter were a huge ball of clay, you could make all the other planets out of it – and still have plenty left over.

The volume of Jupiter is about 1,500,000,000,000,000 cubic km (367,021,930,000,000 cubic miles). The combined volume of the other eight planets is only about two-thirds this amount.

The Great Red Spot of Jupiter is 40,000 km (24,856 miles) wide – wider than three Earths.

Like a huge hurricane

Jupiter has a swirling atmosphere of hydrogen, with weather patterns that can be seen from Earth. The Great Red Spot on Jupiter is a gigantic storm that is more than 300 years old, and more than three times as big as Earth.

A very big valley

Even the great canyons of the USA are minute when compared with the biggest valley on Mars. The Mariner Valley, on Mars, is nine times longer than the Grand Canyon, and three times as deep as Kings Canyon. In fact, it is deep enough and wide enough to swallow the highest peak in South America, Mt Aconcagua.

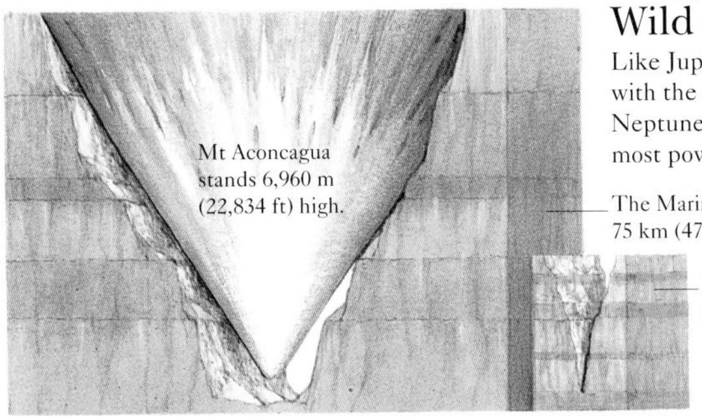

Mt Aconcagua stands 6,960 m (22,834 ft) high.

Wild is the wind on Neptune

Like Jupiter, Neptune has a violent weather system, with the strongest winds of any planet. Winds on Neptune blow more than four times faster than the most powerful tornado recorded on Earth.

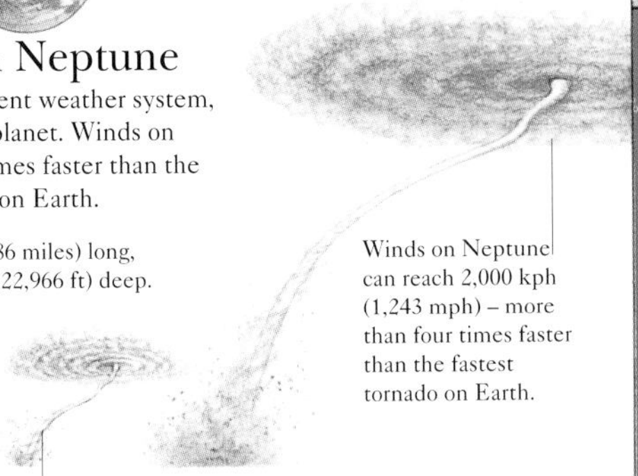

The Mariner Valley is 4,000 km (2,486 miles) long, 75 km (47 miles) wide, and 7,000 m (22,966 ft) deep.

Kings Canyon is 2,449 m (8,199 ft) deep.

Winds on Neptune can reach 2,000 kph (1,243 mph) – more than four times faster than the fastest tornado on Earth.

Tornadoes whirling at up to 450 kph (280 mph) have been recorded on Earth.

...3.3 Saturns

...or 18.5 Neptunes

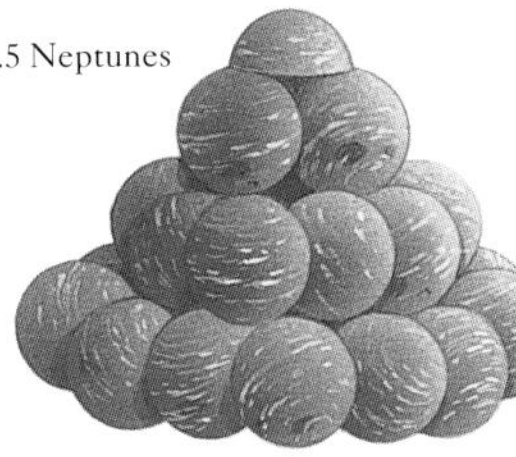

...or 21.9 Uranuses

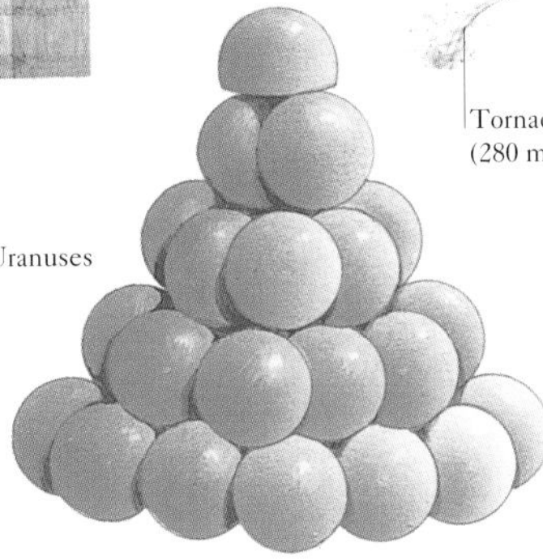

...or 317 Earths

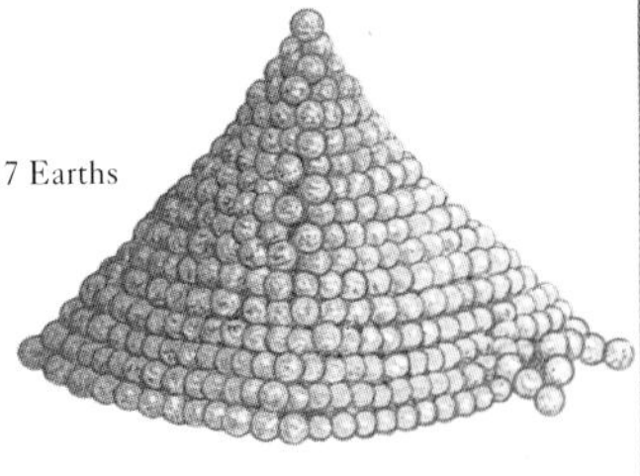

...or 393 Venuses

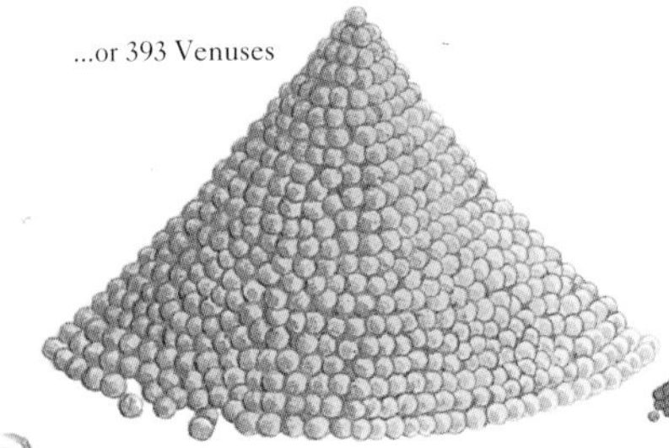

...or 2,894 Marses

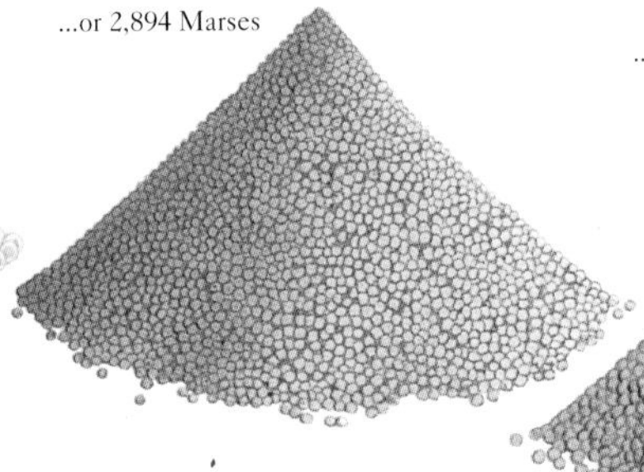

...or 5,788 Mercurys

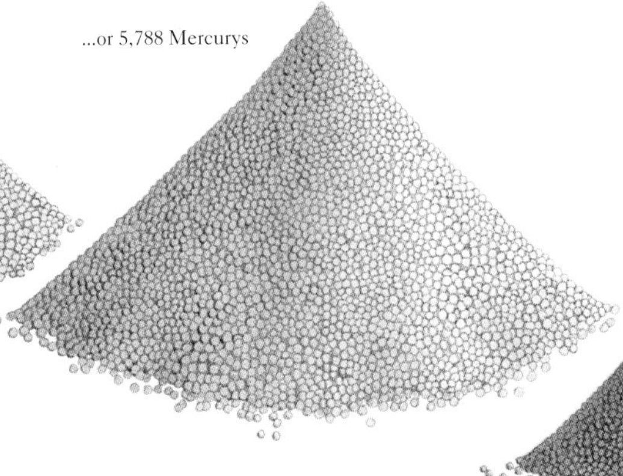

...or 145,796 Plutos.

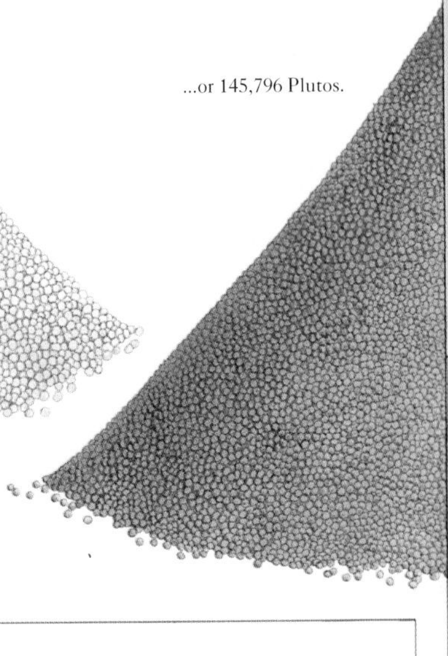

The Sun's spotty face

The temperature of the Sun's surface is about 5,500°C (9,932°F). Strong magnetic fields sometimes restrict the flow of heat from the Sun's interior, creating slightly cooler, darker surface regions, known as sunspots. Sunspots can last for several months and can grow as large as Jupiter.

It would take more than 100 times as many people holding hands to encircle the Sun as it would to go around the equator of the Earth.

1,100,000 km (683,527 miles)

1,200,000 km (745,666 miles)

1,300,000 km (807,805 miles)

1,400,000 km (869,943 miles)

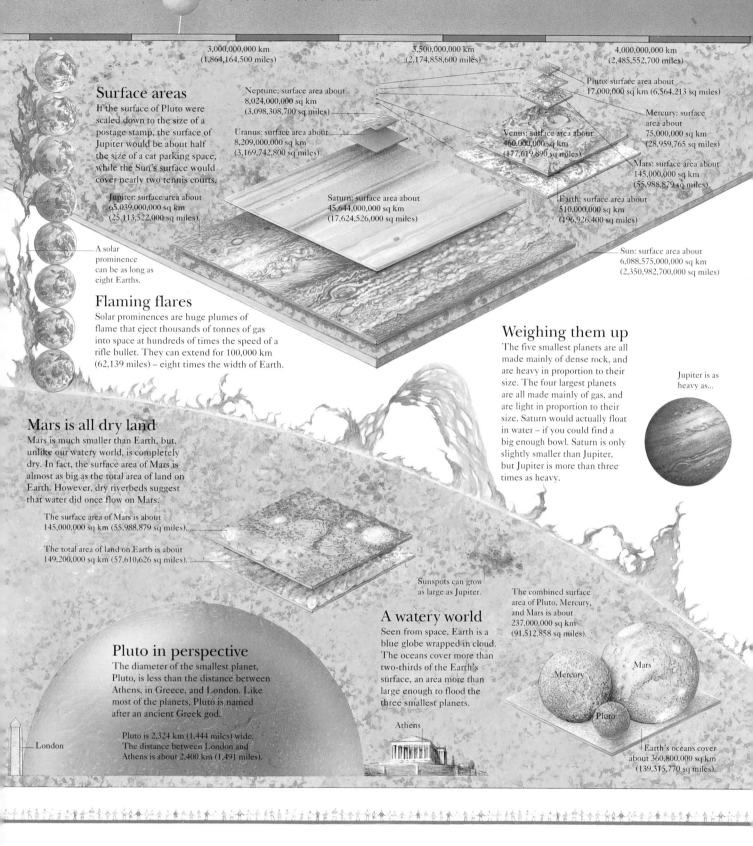

Uranus: average distance from the Sun
2,870,990,000 km (1,783,999,200 miles)

3,000,000,000 km
(1,864,164,500 miles)

3,500,000,000 km
(2,174,858,600 miles)

4,000,000,000 km
(2,485,552,700 miles)

Surface areas

If the surface of Pluto were scaled down to the size of a postage stamp, the surface of Jupiter would be about half the size of a car parking space, while the Sun's surface would cover nearly two tennis courts.

Neptune: surface area about
8,024,000,000 sq km
(3,098,308,700 sq miles)

Uranus: surface area about
8,209,000,000 sq km
(3,169,742,800 sq miles)

Pluto: surface area about
17,000,000 sq km (6,564,213 sq miles)

Mercury: surface area about
75,000,000 sq km
(28,959,765 sq miles)

Venus: surface area about
460,000,000 sq km
(177,619,890 sq miles)

Mars: surface area about
145,000,000 sq km
(55,988,879 sq miles)

Jupiter: surface area about
65,039,000,000 sq km
(25,113,522,000 sq miles)

Saturn: surface area about
45,644,000,000 sq km
(17,624,526,000 sq miles)

Earth: surface area about
510,000,000 sq km
(196,926,400 sq miles)

A solar prominence can be as long as eight Earths.

Sun: surface area about
6,088,575,000,000 sq km
(2,350,982,700,000 sq miles)

Flaming flares

Solar prominences are huge plumes of flame that eject thousands of tonnes of gas into space at hundreds of times the speed of a rifle bullet. They can extend for 100,000 km (62,139 miles) – eight times the width of Earth.

Weighing them up

The five smallest planets are all made mainly of dense rock, and are heavy in proportion to their size. The four largest planets are all made mainly of gas, and are light in proportion to their size. Saturn would actually float in water – if you could find a big enough bowl. Saturn is only slightly smaller than Jupiter, but Jupiter is more than three times as heavy.

Jupiter is as heavy as...

Mars is all dry land

Mars is much smaller than Earth, but, unlike our watery world, is completely dry. In fact, the surface area of Mars is almost as big as the total area of land on Earth. However, dry riverbeds suggest that water did once flow on Mars.

The surface area of Mars is about
145,000,000 sq km (55,988,879 sq miles).

The total area of land on Earth is about
149,200,000 sq km (57,610,626 sq miles).

Sunspots can grow as large as Jupiter.

The combined surface area of Pluto, Mercury, and Mars is about 237,000,000 sq km (91,512,858 sq miles).

A watery world

Seen from space, Earth is a blue globe wrapped in cloud. The oceans cover more than two-thirds of the Earth's surface, an area more than large enough to flood the three smallest planets.

Mars

Mercury

Pluto

Pluto in perspective

The diameter of the smallest planet, Pluto, is less than the distance between Athens, in Greece, and London. Like most of the planets, Pluto is named after an ancient Greek god.

Pluto is 2,324 km (1,444 miles) wide. The distance between London and Athens is about 2,400 km (1,491 miles).

London

Athens

Earth's oceans cover about 360,800,000 sq km (139,315,770 sq miles).

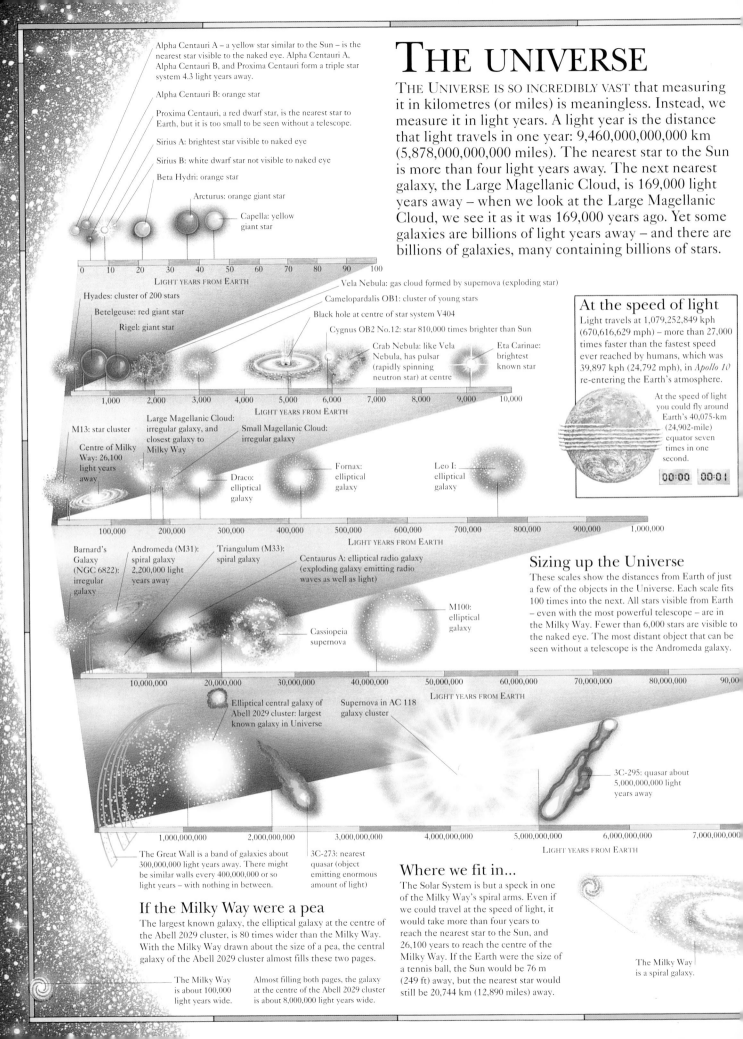

THE UNIVERSE

THE UNIVERSE IS SO INCREDIBLY VAST that measuring it in kilometres (or miles) is meaningless. Instead, we measure it in light years. A light year is the distance that light travels in one year: 9,460,000,000,000 km (5,878,000,000,000 miles). The nearest star to the Sun is more than four light years away. The next nearest galaxy, the Large Magellanic Cloud, is 169,000 light years away – when we look at the Large Magellanic Cloud, we see it as it was 169,000 years ago. Yet some galaxies are billions of light years away – and there are billions of galaxies, many containing billions of stars.

Alpha Centauri A – a yellow star similar to the Sun – is the nearest star visible to the naked eye. Alpha Centauri A, Alpha Centauri B, and Proxima Centauri form a triple star system 4.3 light years away.

Alpha Centauri B: orange star

Proxima Centauri, a red dwarf star, is the nearest star to Earth, but it is too small to be seen without a telescope.

Sirius A: brightest star visible to naked eye

Sirius B: white dwarf star not visible to naked eye

Beta Hydri: orange star

Arcturus: orange giant star

Capella: yellow giant star

LIGHT YEARS FROM EARTH
0 10 20 30 40 50 60 70 80 90 100

Vela Nebula: gas cloud formed by supernova (exploding star)

Hyades: cluster of 200 stars

Camelopardalis OB1: cluster of young stars

Betelgeuse: red giant star

Black hole at centre of star system V404

Rigel: giant star

Cygnus OB2 No.12: star 810,000 times brighter than Sun

Crab Nebula: like Vela Nebula, has pulsar (rapidly spinning neutron star) at centre

Eta Carinae: brightest known star

LIGHT YEARS FROM EARTH
1,000 2,000 3,000 4,000 5,000 6,000 7,000 8,000 9,000 10,000

At the speed of light
Light travels at 1,079,252,849 kph (670,616,629 mph) – more than 27,000 times faster than the fastest speed ever reached by humans, which was 39,897 kph (24,792 mph), in *Apollo 10* re-entering the Earth's atmosphere.

At the speed of light you could fly around Earth's 40,075-km (24,902-mile) equator seven times in one second.

00:00 00:01

M13: star cluster

Large Magellanic Cloud: irregular galaxy, and closest galaxy to Milky Way

Small Magellanic Cloud: irregular galaxy

Centre of Milky Way: 26,100 light years away

Draco: elliptical galaxy

Fornax: elliptical galaxy

Leo I: elliptical galaxy

LIGHT YEARS FROM EARTH
100,000 200,000 300,000 400,000 500,000 600,000 700,000 800,000 900,000 1,000,000

Barnard's Galaxy (NGC 6822): irregular galaxy

Andromeda (M31): spiral galaxy 2,200,000 light years away

Triangulum (M33): spiral galaxy

Centaurus A: elliptical radio galaxy (exploding galaxy emitting radio waves as well as light)

M100: elliptical galaxy

Cassiopeia supernova

Sizing up the Universe
These scales show the distances from Earth of just a few of the objects in the Universe. Each scale fits 100 times into the next. All stars visible from Earth – even with the most powerful telescope – are in the Milky Way. Fewer than 6,000 stars are visible to the naked eye. The most distant object that can be seen without a telescope is the Andromeda galaxy.

LIGHT YEARS FROM EARTH
10,000,000 20,000,000 30,000,000 40,000,000 50,000,000 60,000,000 70,000,000 80,000,000 90,000,000

Elliptical central galaxy of Abell 2029 cluster: largest known galaxy in Universe

Supernova in AC 118 galaxy cluster

3C-295: quasar about 5,000,000,000 light years away

LIGHT YEARS FROM EARTH
1,000,000,000 2,000,000,000 3,000,000,000 4,000,000,000 5,000,000,000 6,000,000,000 7,000,000,000

The Great Wall is a band of galaxies about 300,000,000 light years away. There might be similar walls every 400,000,000 or so light years – with nothing in between.

3C-273: nearest quasar (object emitting enormous amount of light)

Where we fit in...
The Solar System is but a speck in one of the Milky Way's spiral arms. Even if we could travel at the speed of light, it would take more than four years to reach the nearest star to the Sun, and 26,100 years to reach the centre of the Milky Way. If the Earth were the size of a tennis ball, the Sun would be 76 m (249 ft) away, but the nearest star would still be 20,744 km (12,890 miles) away.

The Milky Way is a spiral galaxy.

If the Milky Way were a pea
The largest known galaxy, the elliptical galaxy at the centre of the Abell 2029 cluster, is 80 times wider than the Milky Way. With the Milky Way drawn about the size of a pea, the central galaxy of the Abell 2029 cluster almost fills these two pages.

The Milky Way is about 100,000 light years wide.

Almost filling both pages, the galaxy at the centre of the Abell 2029 cluster is about 8,000,000 light years wide.

Big Betelgeuse

Stars come in many different sizes. Compared with some stars, the Sun is enormous. Compared with others, it is tiny. The largest known star is the red giant Betelgeuse, some 310 light years away. The diameter of Betelgeuse is about 500 times greater than the diameter of the Sun. If Betelgeuse were the size of a large orange, the Sun would be about the size of the head of a pin.

Betelgeuse: approximate diameter 700,000,000 km (434,971,720 miles)

The Sun: diameter 1,392,140 km (865,059 miles)

A midget among stars

Stars such as the Sun eventually turn into white dwarfs, which are very small, but extremely dense, stars. The Sun is about 250 times wider than the smallest known white dwarf, L362-81, which is almost as small as the Moon.

Earth: diameter 12,756 km (7,926 miles)

The Moon: diameter 3,477 km (2,161 miles)

L362-81: estimated diameter 5,600 km (3,480 miles)

The Sun at the same scale as Earth, L362-81, and the Moon

Core cauldron

Like most stars, the Sun is a huge ball of glowing hydrogen. At the Sun's core, the pressure and temperature are so great that hydrogen atoms fuse to make helium. Every second, at its core, the Sun converts about 540,000,000 tonnes (531,496,000 tons) of hydrogen into helium – a weight equal to about 103.5 Great Pyramids.

The Great Pyramid weighs 5,216,400 tonnes (5,134,252 tons) – so 103.5 Great Pyramids would weigh 539,897,400 tonnes (531,395,000 tons).

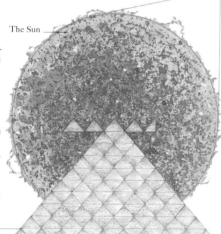

The Sun

Pincredibly dense

Massive stars such as Betelgeuse eventually turn into neutron stars, which are even smaller and denser than white dwarf stars. A neutron star is so dense that just a pinhead-size amount of one might weigh as much as three Empire State Buildings.

The Empire State Building weighs 331,122 tonnes (325,907 tons) – so three Empire State Buildings would weigh 993,366 tonnes (977,722 tons).

A pinhead-size piece of a neutron star might weigh 1,000,000 tonnes (984,200 tons).

Siriusly heavy

The diameter of the Sun is 144 times greater than the diameter of the white dwarf star Sirius B, which is even smaller than Earth. Sirius B is so dense, however, that it actually weighs more than the Sun, which is itself some 330,000 times heavier than Earth.

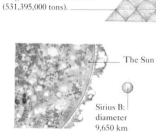

The Sun

Sirius B: diameter 9,650 km (5,996 miles)

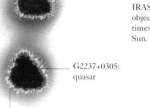

100,000,000

G2237+0305: quasar

IRAS F10214+4724 is an object 300,000,000,000,000 times brighter than the Sun. It is probably a galaxy.

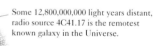

Some 12,800,000,000 light years distant, radio source 4C41.17 is the remotest known galaxy in the Universe.

PC 1247+3406, a quasar, is about 13,200,000,000 light years away, making it the remotest known object in the Universe.

The observable horizon – the edge of the known Universe – is about 14,000,000,000 light years away.

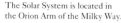

| 000,000,000 | 9,000,000,000 | 10,000,000,000 | 11,000,000,000 | 12,000,000,000 | 13,000,000,000 | 14,000,000,000 | 15,000,000,000 |

The Solar System is located in the Orion Arm of the Milky Way.

Plenty to go around

Nobody knows for sure, but there are an estimated 100,000,000,000 stars in the Milky Way, and about the same number of galaxies in the Universe. That is enough for you and every other person on Earth to stake a claim for 18 of each.

There are an estimated 18 stars in the Milky Way for each person on Earth.

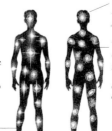

I'll take eight spiral, six elliptical, and four irregular, please.

There are an estimated 18 galaxies in the Universe for each person on Earth.

WATER

WE LIVE IN A WET, wet world. Oceans cover more than two-thirds of our planet's surface. Seen from space, some views of Earth show almost no land at all. The largest ocean, the Pacific, covers nearly a third of the globe and holds about half its water. In fact, 98 per cent of all our world's water is in the sea. Most of the rest is locked up in the two great polar icecaps. Lakes hold just one five-thousandth of our world's water, rivers and streams even less. Clouds hold the least water of all – though you wouldn't think so if you were caught in a tropical rain storm without an umbrella!

Each side of this pool would be about as long as the distance between Perth, in Australia, and New York.

The Moon is 3,477 km (2,161 miles) wide. It would take at least 25 Moons to cover the surface of all the oceans.

Pooled together

Spread out with straight edges, like a swimming pool, all the world's oceans would form a square with sides about 19,000 km (11,806 miles) long – more than five times the diameter of the Moon.

All tanked up

The vast Pacific Ocean contains more water than all the world's other seas and oceans put together. A square tank big enough to hold it would have sides 886 km (551 miles) long.

The Pacific Ocean holds 696,000,000 cubic km (167,000,000 cubic miles) of water.

Lake Nyasa, Malawi/Mozambique: 706 m (2,316 ft)

Lake Baikal: 1,620 m (5,315 ft)

North Sea: 660 m (2,165 ft)

Lake Superior, USA/Canada: 9 m (30 ft)

Plumbing the depths

The world's deepest freshwater lake, Russia's Lake Baikal, reaches 1,620 m (5,315 ft) at its deepest point. The mud at the bottom of the lake is even deeper. Compared with the deepest points in the world's oceans and seas, however, Lake Baikal is shallow. The deepest place on Earth is the Marianas Trench in the Pacific Ocean.

It would take more than 100 Mt Everests stacked on top of one another to reach the surface of this tank.

Gulf of Mexico: 3,787 m (12,425 ft)

South China Sea: 5,016 m (16,456 ft)

Caribbean Sea: 6,946 m (22,788 ft)

Indian Ocean: 7,455 m (24,460 ft)

The Statue of Liberty, in New York, is 93 m (305 ft) high. If all the world's ice melted, poor Liberty would drown – only her torch would show above the waves.

About 71 per cent of the Earth's surface is water.

Atlantic Ocean: 9,219 m (30,246 ft)

Present sea level

It would take a stack of 29 Empire State Buildings to reach the surface of the sea from the bottom of the Marianas Trench.

Rising damp

Only a small proportion of our world's water is locked up in glaciers and the two polar icecaps, but if they all melted, sea levels would rise dramatically – by about 80 m (262 ft).

Marianas Trench, Pacific Ocean: 10,918 m (35,820 ft)

Only 29 per cent of the Earth's surface is land.

Land and sea

The oceans dominate the Earth's surface, just 29 per cent of which is above sea level. Global warming would reduce the land area still further because melting ice would raise sea levels, flooding low-lying coastal land.

On the crest of a wave

Ordinary sea waves are whipped up by the wind. The highest wave ever recorded was in the Pacific Ocean in 1933 and measured 34 m (112 ft) from trough to crest.

Sea tops lake stakes

The landlocked Caspian Sea is the world's largest lake by area, but it is slightly salty. The largest freshwater lake by area is Lake Superior, one of the Great Lakes, in North America.

Lake Baikal: 31,494 sq km (12,160 sq miles)

Aral Sea, Kazakhstan/Uzbekistan: 40,000 sq km (15,444 sq miles)

Lake Victoria, East Africa: 62,940 sq km (24,301 sq miles)

Lake Superior, USA/Canada: 82,260 sq km (31,761 sq miles)

Caspian Sea, Europe/Asia: 378,400 sq km (146,101 sq miles)

The 323,000,000 cubic km (77,000,000 cubic miles) of the Atlantic Ocean would fill a square tank with 686-km (426-mile) sides.

A square tank holding the 284,000,000 cubic km (68,000,000 cubic miles) of the Indian Ocean would need to have sides 657 km (408 miles) long.

Tall fallers

The world's highest waterfall, Angel Falls, in Venezuela, is 979 m (3,212 ft) tall. The longest single drop on the falls is a more modest 807 m (2,648 ft), but that is still more than twice the height of the Eiffel Tower.

Angel Falls, Venezuela: 979 m (3,212 ft)

Utigård, Norway: 800 m (2,625 ft)

Yosemite, USA: 739 m (2,425 ft)

Eiffel Tower: 321 m (1,052 ft)

Sutherland, New Zealand: 580 m (1,903 ft)

Victoria Falls, Zambia/Zimbabwe: 108 m (354 ft)

Niagara Falls, USA/Canada: 51 m (167 ft)

Seawater: 97.2 per cent

Ice: 2.15 per cent

All other water: 0.65 per cent

Almost all at sea

Seawater and ice make up 99.35 per cent of all the Earth's water. Almost all of the rest is groundwater stored in porous rocks. Lakes, rivers, and water in the atmosphere make up only 0.0015 per cent of the Earth's water – a quarter of a teaspoonful for each bathful of seawater.

Owen Falls: 205 cubic km (49 cubic miles)

Aswan, Egypt: 168 cubic km (40 cubic miles)

Guri, Venezuela: 136 cubic km (33 cubic miles)

Zeya, Russia: 68 cubic km (16 cubic miles)

Puddles by comparison

Compared with natural lakes, even the largest artificial reservoirs seem like puny efforts. Lake Baikal, the world's largest freshwater lake by volume, would fill Uganda's Owen Falls, the world's biggest artificial reservoir, 112 times.

Daily output of water from the Amazon

Water in Lake Baikal

Lake Superior: 12,174 cubic km (2,921 cubic miles)

Lake Baikal: 22,995 cubic km (5,519 cubic miles)

Amazing Amazon

The Amazon River, in Brazil, discharges about 10.5 cubic km (2.5 cubic miles) of water a minute into the Atlantic Ocean. That is enough for everyone in the world to have a bath every 44 minutes, allowing 80 litres (17.5 gallons) per bath. If the Amazon drained Lake Baikal, the lake would be two-thirds empty in just one day.

Hidden depths

Although it appears quite small in area, Lake Baikal is extremely deep and contains more water than any other freshwater lake. Lake Superior, the biggest freshwater lake by area, looks bigger, but holds a much smaller volume of water.

Shock waves

Earthquakes and volcanoes can cause especially big waves called tsunamis. The tallest recorded tsunami reached the remarkable height of 85 m (278 ft).

Ahoy there! I'm on this yacht, but I'm so small you can hardly see me.

MOUNTAINS

THE WORLD'S HIGHEST natural features, the great mountains, dwarf even the biggest buildings. The tallest mountain of all is Mt Everest, in the Himalayas. The air at the top of Everest is three times as thin as the air at sea level. What with the numbing cold, thin air, and icy rock faces, it takes even the best prepared and most experienced climbers weeks to reach the top of Everest.

On top of the world

The 35 highest mountains in the world are all in the Himalayan and Karakoram ranges, between China and the Indian subcontinent. The top five are Everest, K2, Kanchenjunga, Lhotse I, and Makalu I. Everest is 27 times as high as the Eiffel Tower. An office building the same height would have at least 2,000 floors.

Everest: 8,848 m (29,028 ft)
K2: 8,611 m (28,250 ft)
Kanchenjunga: 8,597 m (28,208 ft)
Lhotse I: 8,511 m (27,923 ft)
Makalu I: 8,481 m (27,824 ft)

At 8,848 m (29,028 ft), Mt Everest towers over the tallest volcanoes. It is half as high again as Mt Kilimanjaro, more than twice as high as Mt Fuji, and nearly seven times as high as Mt Vesuvius.

Mt Kilimanjaro, in Tanzania, rises to 5,896 m (19,344 ft), making it the highest point in Africa.

Mt Fuji is the highest peak in Japan at 3,776 m (12,388 ft).

Mt Vesuvius, in Italy, is 1,277 m (4,190 ft) high.

Mt Aconcagua, in the Andes, is the highest mountain in the Americas at 6,960 m (22,834 ft).

Everest dwarfs volcanoes

Even the highest volcanoes, such as Mt Kilimanjaro, fall short of Mt Everest. Size is relative, however – although Kilimanjaro is 2,952 m (9,685 ft) shorter than Everest, Kilimanjaro is still 40 times higher than the Great Pyramid, in Egypt.

Helen blows her top

Mt St Helen's, a volcano in Washington state, in the USA, erupted in 1980, throwing huge clouds of ash high into the sky. The ash devastated about 550 sq km (210 sq miles), an area the size of more than 2,100 tennis courts. Before the eruption the volcano was some 2,950 m (9,678 ft) high; afterwards it was about 400 m (1,310 ft) shorter.

Sunken volcano

Mauna Kea   Mt Everest

Mauna Kea is a volcano in Hawaii. Its base is on the seabed. Measured from there, rather than from sea level, it is 1,355 m (4,446 ft) taller than Mt Everest.

Mt Elbrus, Russia: 5,642 m (18,510 ft)

Mt Cook is New Zealand's highest peak at 3,754 m (12,316 ft).

Conifer treeline: 2,500 m (8,202 ft)

Broadleaf treeline: 1,200 m (3,937 ft)

Mt St Helen's: 2,550 m (8,366 ft)

Scale (left margin):
9,000 m (29,528 ft)
8,000 m (26,247 ft)
7,000 m (22,966 ft)
6,000 m (19,685 ft)
5,000 m (16,404 ft)
4,000 m (13,123 ft)
3,000 m (9,843 ft)
2,000 m (6,562 ft)
1,000 m (3,281 ft)
0

Mt Everest:
8,848 m
(29,028 ft)

Martian mammoth

The highest volcano in the Solar System
is Olympus Mons, on Mars. It is three
times higher than Mt Everest, and
nine times higher than
Mt Olympus, in Greece.
It is thought to be
extinct.

Mt Everest

Olympus Mons is
about 26,400 m
(86,614 ft) high.

Yaks can live at heights of
more than 6,000 m (19,685 ft).

Edmund Hillary and Sherpa
Tenzing, the first people to
climb Mt Everest, pitched
their base camp at 5,486 m
(18,000 ft).

Mt McKinley, in the
Alaska Range, is the
highest mountain in
the USA at 6,194 m
(20,320 ft).

Vinson Massif, Antarctica:
5,140 m (16,864 ft)

The air at altitude

The higher you climb, the colder the air
becomes – the temperature falls about 6°C
(11°F) every 1,000 m (3,281 ft). Climbers
wear special clothing to keep warm. The
air also becomes thinner. This means there
is less oxygen in each lungful of air.
Climbers either allow time for their bodies
to adapt, or take extra oxygen supplies.

*I'm level with Hillary
and Tenzing's base
camp on Everest. Even
here the air is twice as
thin as at sea level, and
it's hard to breathe.*

The Matterhorn, in
the European Alps,
is 4,478 m (14,691 ft)
above sea level.

Mont Blanc, in the
European Alps:
4,807 m (15,770 ft)

Toverkop,
in South
Africa, rises
to 2,330 m
(7,644 ft).

Tall buildings (see pages 48-49), at the same scale as the mountains. Even
Toverkop is nearly four times as tall as the world's tallest artificial structure,
the 629-m (2,063-ft) KTHI-TV mast, in North Dakota, USA.

9,000 m
(29,528 ft)

8,000 m
(26,247 ft)

7,000 m
(22,966 ft)

6,000 m
(19,685 ft)

5,000 m
(16,404 ft)

4,000 m
(13,123 ft)

3,000 m
(9,843 ft)

2,000 m
(6,562 ft)

1,000 m
(3,281 ft)

0

GREAT LENGTHS

"IT'S HUGE! COLOSSAL! GINORMOUS!" How do you describe something so huge that it makes you dizzy just to look at it? Countless words have been written about the world's great natural wonders, but nothing can prepare you for the awe-inspiring experience of seeing them for the first time. No structures built by us humans can match nature's greatest marvels, but some of them are still pretty impressive – for example, you could drive around the USA at top speed night and day for four years and still not cover every stretch of road.

Bumble Bee Two – world's smallest biplane: wingspan 1.68 m (5 ft 6 in)

Baby Bird – world's smallest monoplane: wingspan 1.91 m (6 ft 3 in)

Albatross: wingspan 3.7 m (12 ft)

Marabou stork: wingspan 4 m (13 ft)

Silver Bullet – world's smallest jet plane: wingspan 5.2 m (17 ft)

Winged wonders of the world

A biplane (double-winged plane) called *Bumble Bee Two*, built in the 1980s by Robert H. Starr of Arizona, had a wingspan no wider than the outstretched arms of its pilot. At the other extreme, you could park 50 cars side by side on the wings of *Spruce Goose*, a flying-boat built in the USA in the 1940s by Howard Hughes, an eccentric billionaire. *Spruce Goose* barely made it into the air on its maiden flight, and covered a distance less than 10 times its own wingspan. It has not flown since and is now on display at a museum (a very big one).

USA – road network: 6,420,000 km (3,990,056 miles)

India – road network: 2,060,000 km (1,280,298 miles)

Brazil – road network: 1,980,000 km (1,230,577 miles)

USA – rail network: 240,000 km (149,133 miles)

Russia – rail network: 154,000 km (95,711 miles)

China – waterways: 138,600 km (86,124 miles)

Russia – waterways: 101,000 km (62,771 miles)

Canada – rail network: 72,963 km (45,346 miles)

Brazil – waterways: 50,000 km (31,069 miles)

All around the world – and the Sun

The rail network of the USA could go around the Earth's equator almost six times – yet it is tiny compared with the USA's road network. This is so vast that it could go all the way around the Sun's equator – then part of the way around again (although you would need heatproof tyres and a strong nerve to brave the melting tarmac).

The Earth's equator: 40,075 km (24,902 miles)

On the road

The webs of roads and railways that criss-cross the globe are perhaps the biggest objects ever built. The road network of the USA tops the league – you could drive around the USA at 161 kph (100 mph), the top speed of a family car, non-stop for four years and still not cover every stretch of road. You would pass plenty of other cars, though: there are more than 141,000,000 cars in the USA – one for every 44 m (144 ft) of road.

The 240,000-km (149,133-mile) rail network of the USA could go almost six times around the equator of the Earth. By comparison, the world's shortest rail network goes almost nowhere – Vatican City, the world's smallest state, has just 850 m (2,789 ft) of track.

USA – rail network: 240,000 km (149,133 miles)

The Earth's equator: 40,075 km (24,902 miles)

The Grand Canyon averages 1.6 km (1 mile) deep and is 446 km (277 miles) long. Eroding a layer of rock the thickness of a credit card every five years, it took the Colorado River about 10,000,000 years to excavate the gorge – an astonishingly short time in geological terms.

Sliding slowly towards the sea, the Lambert-Fischer Glacier, Antarctica, is 515 km (320 miles) long.

The Mammoth Cave system, the world's most extensive, is 567 km (352 miles) long and riddles Kentucky with holes, like a Swiss cheese.

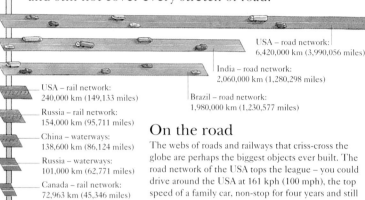

Naturally very long

The longest of the Earth's natural features – the great rivers and mountain ranges – are truly colossal. The longest of all stretches almost from pole to pole, but is entirely hidden from sight – it is the Mid-Atlantic Ridge, a huge underwater mountain range running the full length of the Atlantic Ocean.

Made of coral and home to a huge variety of fish and other marine animals, the Great Barrier Reef stretches for 2,028 km (1,260 miles) along the coast of Queensland, Australia.

Martian metro

The world's largest metropolitan railway has enough track to cover the length of the base of the biggest mountain in the Solar System.

Olympus Mons, Mars: 600 km (373 miles) from end to end

Metropolitan railway system, Tokyo, Japan: 629 km (391 miles)

The Himalayas, Karakorams, and Hindu Kush together form an unbroken mountain range that is 3,862 km (2,400 miles) long.

The Mekong River winds 4,350 km (2,703 miles) through China, Laos, Thailand, Cambodia, and Vietnam before flowing into the South China Sea.

The Chiang Jiang River, in China, is 6,300 km (3,915 miles) long and carries half the country's riverboat traffic.

Fossil remains of *Quetzalcoatlus*, a flying dinosaur that lived 70,000,000 years ago, suggest that it had a wingspan of about 12 m (39 ft).

A Boeing 747 jumbo jet has a wingspan of 59.6 m (195.5 ft) – wider than the Leaning Tower of Pisa is tall.

Spruce Goose Hughes H.4 Hercules flying-boat: wingspan 97.5 m (320 ft)

Spruce Goose: wingspan 97.5 m (320 ft)

Statue of Liberty: 93 m (305 ft) tall

Big bird bigger than Liberty

If the giant flying-boat *Spruce Goose* took off from New York Harbour and made a steeply banked turn around the Statue of Liberty, the tip of one wing would scrape the waves while the tip of the other wing was still above the torch.

Big bridges

The world's deepest lake could not cover the world's longest suspension bridge, the 2,220-m (7,283-ft) Humber Bridge, in the UK – but it would just cover the smaller Severn Bridge.

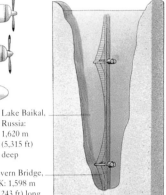

Lake Baikal, Russia: 1,620 m (5,315 ft) deep

Severn Bridge, UK: 1,598 m (5,243 ft) long

Hi there! I'm hitching my way across the good ol' US of A – with a ruck-sack full of road maps on my back...

USA – rail network: 240,000 km (149,133 miles)

USA – road network: 6,283,868 km (3,904,721 miles)

Sun's equator: 4,374,000 km (2,717,952 miles)

Linking the world

Laying telephone cables and oil pipelines is easier and cheaper than digging road and rail tunnels, which therefore tend to be much shorter.

First transatlantic telephone cable: 3,138 km (1,950 miles)

World's longest oil pipeline – Alberta, Canada, to New York: 2,856 km (1,775 miles)

London to Paris: 342 km (213 miles)

World's longest tunnel – water supply tunnel from New York City to Delaware, USA: 169 km (105 miles)

World's longest railway tunnel – Seikan, Japan: 53.9 km (33.5 miles)

English Channel railway tunnel from the UK to France: 50 km (31 miles)

Metropolitan railway tunnel, Moscow, Russia (Kalushskaya line): 37.9 km (23.5 miles)

World's longest road tunnel, St Gotthard, Switzerland: 16.3 km (10 miles)

Entire coastline of New Zealand: 13,134 km (8,161 miles)

Cable across the sea

The longest telecommunications cable in the world runs across the bottom of the Pacific Ocean and links New Zealand and Australia to Canada. It is longer than New Zealand's coastline.

ANZCAN telecommunications cable: 15,151 km (9,415 miles)

Berlin

New York

At 6,448 km (4,007 miles), the Amazon River is longer than the distance from New York to Berlin – 6,385 km (3,968 miles).

At 7,242 km (4,500 miles), the Andes mountain range is longer than the distance from London to Bombay – 7,190 km (4,468 miles).

London

Bombay

At 6,670 km (4,145 miles), the Nile River, in Africa, is the longest in the world.

The Andes mountain range runs like a 7,242-km (4,500-mile) spine down the back of South America.

The Mid-Atlantic Ridge is an 11,300-km (7,022-mile) long mountain range under the sea.

South American wonders

Two of the world's longest natural features are found in South America. The Amazon River is longer than the distance from Berlin, in Germany, to New York, while the Andes mountain range is longer than the distance from Bombay, in India, to London.

St Gotthard road tunnel: 16,320 m (53,543 ft)

Mountain marvel

The St Gotthard road tunnel in the Swiss Alps is the longest in the world. It is almost twice as long as the height of the world's tallest mountain, Mt Everest.

Mt Everest: 8,848 m (29,028 ft)

6,000 km (3,728 miles)   7,000 km (4,350 miles)   8,000 km (4,971 miles)   9,000 km (5,592 miles)   10,000 km (6,214 miles)

WEATHER

WEATHER AFFECTS ALL of our lives, but to a greater or lesser degree depending on where we live. Some parts of the world are safe and fertile places, with comfortable amounts of sunshine, rain, and snow. Others are hot, inhospitable deserts, or frozen Arctic wastes. Then there are the hot and humid tropics – highly fertile lands, but frequently ravaged by mighty storms and floods.

Hurricane force

In summer, islands and coastal countries in the tropics are sometimes hit by severe storms, known as hurricanes in the Gulf of Mexico and Caribbean, cyclones in the Indian Ocean, and typhoons in the north-west Pacific. They can last 10 days or more, with winds of 161 kph (100 mph) – the top speed of a family car. Remarkably, the centre, or eye, of a tropical storm is calm.

Typhoons covering an area larger than that of Bangladesh – 143,998 sq km (55,600 sq miles) – frequently sweep across this country, causing widespread flooding and destruction.

When Hurricane Camille hit the coast of Mississippi and Alabama in the USA in 1969, gusts of 322 kph (200 mph) were recorded – faster than the fastest motorcycle.

Twisting tornadoes

A tornado, or twister, is a rapidly spinning column of air that whirls dust and debris high into the sky and can destroy buildings. Tornadoes at sea are called waterspouts – although short-lived, they can whisk a column of water up to cloud level.

A tornado whirling at 450 kph (280 mph) – faster than Donald Campbell's record-breaking 1964 *Bluebird* speedboat, and nearly as fast as a drag car – struck Wichita Falls, in Texas, in the USA, in 1958.

The Empire State Building is 381 m (1,250 ft) high. A waterspout four times as high, at 1,528 m (5,014 ft), was seen off Australia in 1898.

Bluebird speedboat: 445 kph (277 mph)

Drag car: 497 kph (309 mph)

Continental extremes

A comparison of the greatest extremes of temperature – the hottest and coldest on record for each continent – shows that Oceania has the smallest range and Asia the greatest.

MAXIMUM TEMPERATURE	MINIMUM TEMPERATURE
Oceania: 53°C (127°F)	Oceania: –22°C (–8°F)
South America: 49°C (120°F)	South America: –33°C (–27°F)
Africa: 58°C (136°F)	Africa: –24°C (–11°F)
Antarctica: 14°C (57°F)	Antarctica: –89°C (–128°F)
Europe: 50°C (122°F)	Europe: –55°C (–67°F)
North America: 57°C (135°F)	North America: –63°C (–81°F)
Asia: 54°C (129°F)	Asia: –68°C (–90°F)

The wind and the water

The Beaufort scale of wind speeds is used worldwide in weather reports and forecasts compiled for ships and boats at sea. It was invented in 1805 by British Admiral Sir Francis Beaufort. The scale ranges from Force 0, representing a calm sea, through Force 8, representing a gale, to Force 12 and above, signifying hurricane-strength winds.

0 – calm: 0-2 kph (0-1 mph)
1 – light air: 2-5 kph (1-3 mph)
2 – light breeze: 6-11 kph (4-7 mph)
3 – gentle breeze: 12-19 kph (8-12 mph)
4 – moderate breeze: 20-29 kph (12-18 mph)
5 – fresh breeze: 30-38 kph (19-24 mph)
6 – strong breeze: 39-50 kph (24-31 mph)
7 – high wind: 51-61 kph (32-38 mph)
8 – gale: 62-74 kph (38-46 mph)

Fire and ice

Between the fiery surface of the Sun and the absolute cold of space there is only a narrow band of temperatures where life is possible. Even within this narrow band there are huge variations, however – from the searing heat of some deserts to the icy polar wastes.

Cloncurry, Australia, has recorded temperatures as high as 52.8°C (127°F).

The highest temperature ever recorded in the shade – 57.8°C (136°F), at al'Aziziyah, in the Libyan desert, in September 1922 – was hot enough to fry an egg.

The top summer temperature in Rome, Italy, is a hot but tolerable 40°C (104°F).

Over the period 1960-66 an average temperature of 34.4°C (94°F) was recorded for Dallol, in Ethiopia – the hottest on Earth.

Fresh water freezes at 0°C (32°F) at sea level.

A comfortable room temperature is considered to be 20°C (68°F).

That's much better!

The surface of the Sun is a scorching 5,330°C (9,626°F).

At sea level, fresh water boils at 100°C (212°F).

The temperature at the bottom of the world's deepest mines reaches 73°C (163°F).

100°C (212°F)   80°C (176°F)   60°C (140°F)   40°C (104°F)   20°C (68°F)

Clouds in the sky

The lowest clouds, stratus, form below 460 m (1,509 ft) – not much higher than the world's tallest office building, the 452-m (1,482-ft) high Petronas Towers, in Kuala Lumpur, Malaysia. The highest clouds, cirrus, can be seen at 13,700 m (44,948 ft) – nearly 5,000 m (16,404 ft) higher than the world's highest mountain.

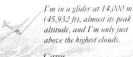

I'm in a glider at 14,000 m (45,932 ft), almost its peak altitude, and I'm only just above the highest clouds.

Cirrus

Cirrostratus

Cumulonimbus

Cirrocumulus

Mt Everest: 8,848 m (29,028 ft)

Altocumulus

Altostratus

Cumulonimbus

Nimbostratus

Stratocumulus

Cumulus

Stratus

Fog

14,000 m (45,932 ft)

13,000 m (42,651 ft)

12,000 m (39,370 ft)

11,000 m (36,089 ft)

10,000 m (32,808 ft)

9,000 m (29,528 ft)

8,000 m (26,247 ft)

7,000 m (22,966 ft)

6,000 m (19,685 ft)

5,000 m (16,404 ft)

4,000 m (13,123 ft)

3,000 m (9,843 ft)

2,000 m (6,562 ft)

1,000 m (3,281 ft)

0

Lightning strikes

The Earth is struck by lightning 100 times a second. High-speed photography shows that each strike consists of a lead stroke and a return stroke. The lead stroke travels at 160-1,600 km (99-994 miles) per second and forks as it opens a channel from the clouds to the ground. The much brighter return stroke flashes up this channel at about 140,000 km (86,994 miles) per second, or nearly half the speed of light.

Lightning can extend up to 32 km (20 miles). A space shuttle takes only 100 seconds to travel this high from lift-off, but the return stroke of a lightning bolt is more than 400,000 times as fast.

A typical lightning bolt is about 800 m (2,625 ft) long – almost three times the height of the Eiffel Tower, which is 321 m (1,052 ft).

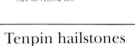

Leaning Tower of Pisa: 55 m (180 ft)

In the 12 months from 19 February 1971 to 18 February 1972, 31 m (102 ft) of snow fell on Mt Rainier in the USA.

Tamarac, California: 11.4 m (37 ft 5 in) of snow in March 1911

New York receives an average of 74 cm (2 ft 5 in) of snow every year.

Tenpin hailstones

On 3 September 1970, hailstones up to 760 g (1 lb 11 oz) in weight and up to 20 cm (8 in) in diameter – as big as tenpin bowling balls – fell at Coffeyville, Kansas, in the USA.

Snowed under

There are records of nearly 2 m (6.5 ft) of snow falling in one day – enough to bury a standing adult. Single snowstorms have resulted in falls of almost 5 m (16 ft) – enough to cover three adults standing on each other's shoulders. In 12 months, enough snow falls on the world's snowiest place, Mt Rainier, in Washington state, in the USA, to bury more than half of the Leaning Tower of Pisa.

Rain around the world

Annual rainfall varies greatly worldwide. Aswan, Egypt, has a measly 0.5 mm (0.02 in). However, Bonaventura, Colombia, has a drenching 6.7 m (22 ft) – enough to cover almost four adults standing on each other's shoulders. Meanwhile, at Mt Waialeale, Hawaii, it rains on up to 350 days every year.

Cilaos, La Réunion, Indian Ocean, 15-16 March 1952 – highest ever rainfall in 24 hours: 1.87 m (6 ft 2 in)

Madrid, Spain: average annual rainfall 42 cm (16.5 in)

Cherrapunji, Assam, India, 1 August 1860-31 July 1861 – highest annual total rainfall : 26.5 m (87 ft)

9 – strong gale: 75-86 kph (47-53 mph)
10 – whole gale: 87-101 kph (54-63 mph)
11 – storm: 102-115 kph (63-71 mph)

9

10

11

12

13

14

15

16

17

12 – hurricane: 116-132 kph (72-82 mph)
13 – hurricane: 133-149 kph (83-93 mph)
14 – hurricane: 150-166 kph (93-103 mph)

15-17: hurricanes of 166-218 kph (103-135 mph)... rarely encountered, but cause massive destruction

Norilsk, Russia, is the coldest inhabited place in the world, with an average temperature of –10.9°C (12.4°F).

At an average –57.8°C (–72°F), Polus Nedostupnosti, in Antarctica, is the coldest place on Earth.

The coldest temperature ever recorded on the surface of the Earth was –89.2°C (–128.6°F), at Vostok, Antarctica, in 1983.

Temperatures in outer space plunge to within 3°C (4°F) of the coldest temperature possible, known as absolute zero: –273.16°C (–459.69°F).

The lowest temperature ever recorded in the upper atmosphere was –143°C (–225°F), 80 km (50 miles) above Kronogard, Sweden, in 1963.

−20°C (−4°F)   −60°C (−76°F)   −100°C (−148°F)   −140°C (−220°F)   −180°C (−292°F)   −220°C (−364°F)   −260°C (−436°F)

DISASTERS

"STOP PRESS – HUNDREDS DIE in earthquake!" "Famine tragedy – thousands starve."
Newspaper headlines and television news flashes like these make us feel mixed emotions:
shock at first, then sympathy as we watch rescue workers and helpers – perhaps even
excitement when we read about lucky escapes. We also feel relieved that we are not
among the victims, especially when the disaster happens close to home. It is easy to think,
"It could have been me." Disasters on the other side of the world have much less impact
on us, even when they are far more catastrophic.

Worldwide, modern tankers
safely carry 60 bathtubs of
crude oil for every teaspoonful
accidentally spilled.

Some 350,000,000 litres (76,990,761 gallons) of
crude oil spilled into the Carribean when the
tankers *Atlantic Empress* and *Aegean Captain*
collided off Trinidad & Tobago in 1979.

Oiling the waters

The largest oil tankers – supertankers – can carry as
much as 650,000,000 litres (142,982,840 gallons) of crude
oil at a time. That is about 4.5 litres (1 gallon) for every
car in the USA, so a major spill can spread over a vast
area of the sea and pollute a huge length of coastline.
However, nothing can ever protect the oceans against
deliberate releases of oil such as the one by Iraq in
1991,during the Gulf War.

In 1978 the tanker
Amoco Cadiz spilled
268,000,000 litres
(58,952,925 gallons) of
crude oil into the sea
off the coast of France.

The explosive eruption
of the volcanic island of
Krakatoa triggered a 37-m
(120-ft) high tsunami, or
giant ocean wave.

In 1991 Iraq deliberately
discharged 1,713,000,000 litres
(376,814,780 gallons) of crude
oil into the Persian Gulf.

When the *Torrey Canyon* ran aground off the coast
of Great Britain in 1967 it spilled 139,000,000 litres
(30,576,330 gallons) of crude oil into the sea.

In 1989 the *Exxon Valdez* spilled 41,000,000 litres
(9,018,918 gallons) of crude oil into the sea off
the coast of Alaska.

Ships left high and dry

The Aral Sea, in Kazakhstan and Uzbekistan, was once the
world's fourth biggest lake. Until the 1960s, 56 cubic km
(13 cubic miles) of water flowed into it each year.
Since the 1960s, 97 per cent of this water
has been diverted for irrigation
and industry. As a result, the
Aral Sea is steadily drying up. An
area the size of Lake Tanganyika, in
Africa, has already been lost. The lake now
covers about half its original area – with ships left rusting
away on dry land, and the lake nowhere in sight.

Aral Sea in 1964:
about 65,500 sq km
(25,292 sq miles)

Aral Sea in 1993:
about 36,500 sq km
(14,094 sq miles)

Krakatoa catastrophe

In 1883 a series of huge blasts blew apart the volcanic island
of Krakatoa, in Indonesia, killing 36,000 people. Heard
some 4,800 km (2,983 miles) away, the blasts ejected
21 cubic km (5 cubic miles) of dust into the
air – more than 8,000 times the
volume of the Great Pyramid.

Sea takes greatest toll

Most of the worst transport disasters
are at sea, but since long-distance
travellers switched to flying,
plane crashes have grabbed
the headlines. This makes
some people afraid of
flying, when in fact
it is one of the
safest forms
of travel.

Challenger space shuttle, USA, 1986:
seven die in explosion shortly after take-off

Hindenburg airship, New Jersey, USA, 1937:
36 die in mooring explosion

Le Mans motor racing circuit, France, 1955:
82 die when car crashes and explodes

New York Subway, 1918:
97 die in train crash

Air India 747, Irish Sea, 1985:
329 die in mid-air aircraft explosion

Japan Air Lines 747, Japan, 1985:
520 die in mountain plane crash

KLM & Pan Am 747s, Canary Islands, 1977:
583 die in airport runway collision

Railway, Bihar, India, 1981:
800 die when train plunges off bridge

Titanic passenger liner, North Atlantic, 1912:
1,517 die in sinking of ship after it hits iceberg

The biggest killers

Disease and famine kill far more people
than wars or natural disasters. The Black
Death killed up to three-quarters of all
people in Europe in the 14th century.
Without modern drugs, a similar plague
today could kill 4,000,000,000 people.

Rat fleas spread the plague
when they bite people.

Black
Death:
75,000,000
die

Malaria, spread by mosquito
bites in the tropics: worldwide,
2,000,000 die each year

Korean War, 1950-53:
1,900,000 die in battle

Irish potato famine,
1846-51:
1,500,000 die

Bangladesh
cyclone, 1970:
1,000,000 die

Famine, China,
1959-61: 30,000,000 die

Influenza, worldwide,
1918: 21,600,000 die

World War II, 1939-45:
16,000,000 die in battle

World War I, 1914-18:
8,500,000 die in battle

Sultana steamboat, Mississippi, 1865:
1,547 die in river boat explosion

Salang Tunnel (road and rail), Afghanistan, 1982:
3,000 die in petrol tanker crash and explosion

Donna Paz ferry, Philippines, 1987:
3,000 die when oil tanker rams ferry

0   1,000 people   2,000 people   3,000 people

Explosive force

Some modern nuclear warheads are 1,250 times as powerful as the atomic bomb dropped on Hiroshima. But the Tunguska explosion was 1,500 times as powerful as the Hiroshima bomb, while the combined force of the four Krakatoa explosions was 10,000 times more powerful.

Hiroshima bomb
Equal to 20,320 tonnes (20,000 tons) of ordinary TNT explosive

Tunguska meteorite
Equal to 30,500,000 tonnes (30,000,000 tons) of TNT

Krakatoa volcano
Equal to 203,000,000 tonnes (200,000,000 tons) of TNT

Tunguska meteorite

Hiroshima atomic bomb

Lava not the real killer

Not all volcanoes kill through sudden explosions or eruptions. In 1783, Laki volcano, in Iceland, spewed out lava – molten rock – for two months. The lava filled two valleys, but killed very few people directly. Most of the 10,000 deaths were caused by sulphurous fumes, and by starvation resulting from volcanic ash killing crops and animals.

The lava was 30 m (98 ft) deep – enough to bury a 20-m (66-ft) four-storey town house.

Siberian shocker

One day in 1908 a blast filled the sky above Tunguska, in Siberia, a remote area of Russia. Heard 1,000 km (621 miles) away, it flattened trees over 5,000 sq km (1,931 sq miles), an area twice the size of Luxembourg, but no-one was killed. Scientists believe a large meteorite exploded as it hit the upper atmosphere.

Hiroshima

In 1945 an atomic bomb was dropped on the city of Hiroshima, in Japan. It killed about 140,000 people and almost totally destroyed the city.

Cone in a cornfield

The 1943 eruption of Parícutin, in Mexico, killed no-one, but as the volcano grew it engulfed a village and destroyed large areas of farmland. It appeared, almost without warning, in a cornfield.

Only the tip of the 553-m (1,815-ft) CN Tower, in Toronto, Canada, would clear the top of the cone.

One day after the cone first appeared it was 10 m (33 ft) high.

Parícutin

Only one year after the cone first appeared it was 450 m (1,476 ft) high. At the peak of its activity it was ejecting 2,440 tonnes (2,400 tons) of material a minute. In 1952 the cone was measured at 528 m (1,732 ft).

China's flood hazard

China's Yellow River regularly floods huge areas of farmland. Heavy rains in 1887 caused it to flood an area one-and-a-half times the size of Ireland. The areas devastated by some of the world's most famous city fires are tiny by comparison.

Great Fire of London, 1666: 1.9 sq km (0.7 sq miles) destroyed

Chicago, 1871: fire destroys 8.9 sq km (3.4 sq miles)

Yellow River, 1887: 125,000 sq km (48,266 sq miles) flooded

Area of Ireland: 83,850 sq km (32,377 sq miles)

Disaster areas

Diseases, such as the plague, can cause worldwide destruction, but most disasters are far less extensive. Those that have the most widespread effects are floods, which can drown small countries. Global warming, caused by atmospheric pollution trapping the Sun's heat, could in future cause worse floods than anything yet seen, as rising sea levels wash over coastal cities.

Bad vibrations

The Richter scale of earthquake size measures how much the ground moves, but is not a guide to the destruction caused – that depends much more on the structure of the rock and earth where the earthquake strikes, and on the construction of the local buildings.

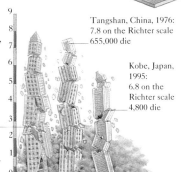

Tangshan, China, 1976: 7.8 on the Richter scale 655,000 die

Kobe, Japan, 1995: 6.8 on the Richter scale 4,800 die

San Francisco, 1906: 8.25 on the Richter scale – about 500 die

Wilhelm Gustloff refugee ship, Baltic Sea, 1945: 7,700 die when torpedoed ship sinks – death toll equal to almost 14 full jumbo jets

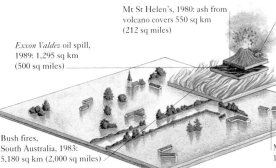

Mt St Helen's, 1980: ash from volcano covers 550 sq km (212 sq miles)

San Francisco, 1906: fire caused by earthquake destroys 12 sq km (4.6 sq miles)

Exxon Valdez oil spill, 1989: 1,295 sq km (500 sq miles)

Bush fires, South Australia, 1983: 5,180 sq km (2,000 sq miles)

Mississippi River, 1927: floods cover 46,600 sq km (17,994 sq miles)

5,000 people   6,000 people   7,000 people   8,000 people

GREAT AND SMALL

COULD ANTS GROW big enough to eat people? Why are the largest animals living today found in the sea, and not on land? The simple answer to such fascinating questions is that animal size is governed by nature. We need not fear the jaws of giant insects, because giant insects would soon suffocate – their simple breathing tubes could not supply them with enough air. Fierce competition for food stops the largest land animals, elephants, from being bigger. When giant dinosaurs roamed the Earth they had no competitors – but they needed legs like tree trunks to support their heavy bodies. The biggest animals today, blue whales, feed freely on almost unlimited supplies of krill, a shrimp-like creature. Whales' bodies are adapted to the buoyancy of the sea – on land, they would be crushed by their own weight.

At up to 5.8 m (19 ft), a fully grown giraffe is so tall that its arteries have special valves to help pump blood up to its head. Without these valves, its heart would have to be as big as its whole body.

Twice as tall as all the rest

The giraffe is by far the tallest animal. It is twice as tall as the African elephant, and more than three times as tall as the average man. Its long legs and long neck allow it to browse on tree-top leaves beyond the reach of even the elephant's long trunk

Adult bull African elephants grow to more than 3 m (10 ft) tall.

Rearing on its hind legs, the grizzly bear of North America can be 3 m (10 ft) tall.

With its long legs and long neck, an ostrich can be 2.7 m (9 ft) tall.

Long gone Jurassic giant

The biggest dinosaurs were plant eaters. They were bigger than any living land animals, because they had no competitors. One of the longest, measured from nose to tip of tail, was *Diplodocus*, which lived on the North American continent some 145,000,000 years ago. *Diplodocus* was nearly three times as long as the longest land animal living today, the reticulated python.

Found in Asia, and growing up to 10.7 m (35 ft) – almost half the length of a tennis court – the reticulated python is the longest snake in the world.

The Nile crocodile grows up to 5 m (16 ft) in length – more than 125 times as long as the world's smallest gecko.

Bull African elephants can be 5 m (16 ft) long – more than 7 m (23 ft) if you include their trunks and tails.

The Giant Indian rhinoceros grows up to 4.3 m (14 ft) long – about the length of a small car.

A dromedary camel can be 3 m (10 ft) long from the end of its nose to the base of its tail.

A tiger can be 2.8 m (9 ft) long – about six times as long as a domestic cat.

At 12 m (39 ft 4 in), the rare, warm-water whale shark is about one-third as long as a blue whale. Luckily for us, it feeds on plankton and is completely harmless.

Including their tentacles, giant deep-sea squid can be up to 17.5 m (57 ft) long.

Gigantic jellyfish

In the buoyant, food-rich world of the sea, animals can grow to enormous sizes. The blue whale has the longest body, but if you include the tentacles, the Arctic giant jellyfish is the longest sea creature of all. Fanned out, its tentacles would form a circle covering an area bigger than 15 tennis courts.

The giant spider crab, found off Japan, has a body about 25 cm (10 in) in diameter but a leg span up to 3.7 m (12 ft).

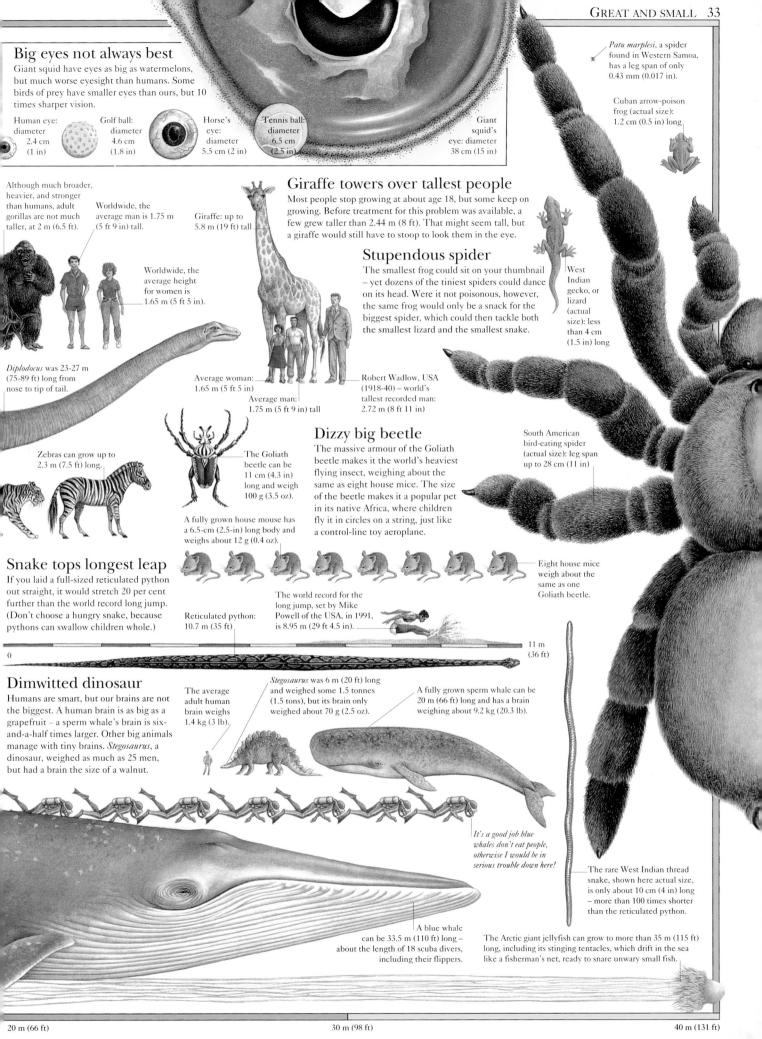

Big eyes not always best

Giant squid have eyes as big as watermelons, but much worse eyesight than humans. Some birds of prey have smaller eyes than ours, but 10 times sharper vision.

Human eye: diameter 2.4 cm (1 in)

Golf ball: diameter 4.6 cm (1.8 in)

Horse's eye: diameter 5.5 cm (2 in)

Tennis ball: diameter 6.5 cm (2.5 in)

Giant squid's eye: diameter 38 cm (15 in)

Patu marplesi, a spider found in Western Samoa, has a leg span of only 0.43 mm (0.017 in).

Cuban arrow-poison frog (actual size): 1.2 cm (0.5 in) long

Giraffe towers over tallest people

Most people stop growing at about age 18, but some keep on growing. Before treatment for this problem was available, a few grew taller than 2.44 m (8 ft). That might seem tall, but a giraffe would still have to stoop to look them in the eye.

Stupendous spider

The smallest frog could sit on your thumbnail – yet dozens of the tiniest spiders could dance on its head. Were it not poisonous, however, the same frog would only be a snack for the biggest spider, which could then tackle both the smallest lizard and the smallest snake.

West Indian gecko, or lizard (actual size): less than 4 cm (1.5 in) long

Although much broader, heavier, and stronger than humans, adult gorillas are not much taller, at 2 m (6.5 ft).

Worldwide, the average man is 1.75 m (5 ft 9 in) tall.

Giraffe: up to 5.8 m (19 ft) tall

Worldwide, the average height for women is 1.65 m (5 ft 5 in).

Diplodocus was 23-27 m (75-89 ft) long from nose to tip of tail.

Average woman: 1.65 m (5 ft 5 in)

Average man: 1.75 m (5 ft 9 in) tall

Robert Wadlow, USA (1918-40) – world's tallest recorded man: 2.72 m (8 ft 11 in)

Zebras can grow up to 2.3 m (7.5 ft) long.

Dizzy big beetle

The massive armour of the Goliath beetle makes it the world's heaviest flying insect, weighing about the same as eight house mice. The size of the beetle makes it a popular pet in its native Africa, where children fly it in circles on a string, just like a control-line toy aeroplane.

The Goliath beetle can be 11 cm (4.3 in) long and weigh 100 g (3.5 oz).

A fully grown house mouse has a 6.5-cm (2.5-in) long body and weighs about 12 g (0.4 oz).

South American bird-eating spider (actual size): leg span up to 28 cm (11 in)

Eight house mice weigh about the same as one Goliath beetle.

Snake tops longest leap

If you laid a full-sized reticulated python out straight, it would stretch 20 per cent further than the world record long jump. (Don't choose a hungry snake, because pythons can swallow children whole.)

Reticulated python: 10.7 m (35 ft)

The world record for the long jump, set by Mike Powell of the USA, in 1991, is 8.95 m (29 ft 4.5 in).

11 m (36 ft)

0

Dimwitted dinosaur

Humans are smart, but our brains are not the biggest. A human brain is as big as a grapefruit – a sperm whale's brain is six-and-a-half times larger. Other big animals manage with tiny brains. *Stegosaurus*, a dinosaur, weighed as much as 25 men, but had a brain the size of a walnut.

The average adult human brain weighs 1.4 kg (3 lb).

Stegosaurus was 6 m (20 ft) long and weighed some 1.5 tonnes (1.5 tons), but its brain only weighed about 70 g (2.5 oz).

A fully grown sperm whale can be 20 m (66 ft) long and has a brain weighing about 9.2 kg (20.3 lb).

It's a good job blue whales don't eat people, otherwise I would be in serious trouble down here!

The rare West Indian thread snake, shown here actual size, is only about 10 cm (4 in) long – more than 100 times shorter than the reticulated python.

A blue whale can be 33.5 m (110 ft) long – about the length of 18 scuba divers, including their flippers.

The Arctic giant jellyfish can grow to more than 35 m (115 ft) long, including its stinging tentacles, which drift in the sea like a fisherman's net, ready to snare unwary small fish.

LIGHT AND HEAVY

SIZE AND WEIGHT do not always go hand in hand. A hummingbird and a golf ball are much the same size, but it takes as many as 28 hummingbirds to equal the weight of one golf ball. The heaviest metal, osmium, weighs more than 40 times as much as the lightest, lithium. The range of weights in both the human and natural worlds is enormous. The world's largest bell, the Tsar Kolokol bell, weighs almost as much as the Statue of Liberty, yet the statue is more than seven times as tall – while the heaviest mammal, the blue whale, can weigh an incredible 90,000,000 times more than the lightest, the pygmy shrew.

From heavy metal to lightweight lithium

The heaviest metal, and the heaviest element, is osmium. A 30-cm (12-in) cube of osmium would weigh about 610 kg (1,345 lb), or as much as 10 adults, each weighing 61 kg (134 lb). A 30-cm (12-in) cube of lithium, the lightest metal, would tip the scales at only 14.4 kg (32 lb) – not much heavier than the average two-year-old boy.

A 30-cm (12-in) cube of osmium would weigh as much as ten 61-kg (134-lb) adults.

The average two-year-old boy weighs 11.8 kg (26 lb).

A 30-cm (12-in) cube of lithium would weigh only 14.4 kg (32 lb).

Where did that rocket come from? Suddenly this tree-climbing lark doesn't seem such a good idea!

The General Sherman giant sequoia is nearly 84 m (276 ft) tall and weighs an estimated 2,500 tonnes (2,461 tons).

Large weight of living wood

The largest living thing on Earth is the General Sherman giant sequoia tree, in Sequoia National Park, California. It weighs an estimated 2,500 tonnes (2,461 tons) – almost as much as a fuel-laden *Saturn V* rocket at lift-off.

At lift-off, a *Saturn V* rocket stood 111 m (364 ft) tall and weighed more than 2,960 tonnes (2,913 tons).

Almost a rocket a storey

Built between 1929 and 1931, the rocket-shaped 102-storey concrete and steel Empire State Building weighs about the same as 112 *Saturn V* rockets at lift-off.

The Empire State Building weighs 331,122 tonnes (325,907 tons).

Altogether, 112 *Saturn V* rockets at lift-off would weigh more than 331,520 tonnes (326,299 tons).

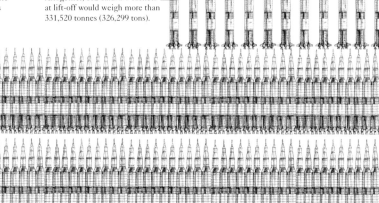

All the hydrogen in *Graf Zeppelin II* weighed less than 18 tonnes (18 tons).

An adult bull African elephant weighs about 5 tonnes (5 tons).

Lighter and heavier than air

Hydrogen is the lightest gas, radon the heaviest. *Graf Zeppelin II*, one of the two largest airships ever built, held almost 200,000 cubic m (7,062,895 cubic ft) of hydrogen, weighing little more than three bull African elephants. Filled with radon, it could not have flown – the gas would have weighed as much as 400 elephants.

Graf Zeppelin II was about 245 m (804 ft) long.

Had *Graf Zeppelin II* been filled with radon, the gas would have weighed more than 2,000 tonnes (1,969 tons) – as much as 400 bull African elephants.

A whale of a rocket

A *Saturn V* rocket at lift-off weighed about the same as 23 fully grown blue whales. Most of the weight was accounted for by three full fuel tanks and three sets of engines, which were fired and jettisoned in succession.

Adult blue whales weigh about 130 tonnes (128 tons) each – so 23 adult blue whales weigh about 2,990 tonnes (2,943 tons).

Saturn V rocket: more than 2,960 tonnes (2,913 tons)

Tower's iron tonnage

Modifications to the Eiffel Tower steadily increased its weight from about 9,700 tonnes (9,547 tons) when it was completed in 1889, but in 1983 it was reduced to its present 8,757 tonnes (8,619 tons) – almost three times the weight of a *Saturn V* rocket at lift-off.

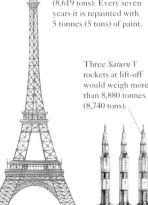

Made of iron, the Eiffel Tower weighs 8,757 tonnes (8,619 tons). Every seven years it is repainted with 5 tonnes (5 tons) of paint.

Three *Saturn V* rockets at lift-off would weigh more than 8,880 tonnes (8,740 tons).

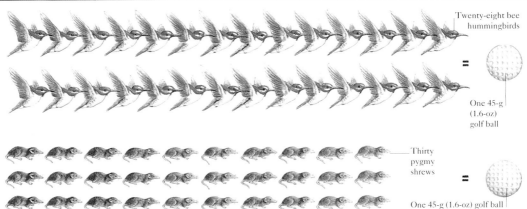

Twenty-eight bee
hummingbirds

=

One 45-g
(1.6-oz)
golf ball

Small for their size...

A bee hummingbird, the world's smallest bird, weighs only about 1.6 g (0.06 oz), while a pygmy shrew, the world's smallest mammal, weighs only about 1.5 g (0.05 oz). Both are about the size of a golf ball, but one 45-g (1.6-oz) golf ball weighs as much as 28 bee hummingbirds or 30 pygmy shrews.

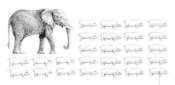

Thirty
pygmy
shrews

=

One 45-g (1.6-oz) golf ball

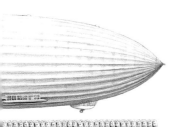

Mammoth mammals

Blue whales are the largest animals on Earth. Nobody has ever managed to weigh one intact, but they grow to an estimated 130 tonnes (128 tons) – about 26 times as heavy as a bull African elephant, the largest animal on land. In turn, a bull African elephant is about 26 times heavier than the average pig. Like pygmy shrews, blue whales are mammals – but they can be an incredible 90,000,000 times as heavy.

The average pig weighs 192 kg (423 lb). A bull African elephant weighs some 5 tonnes (5 tons) – about the same as 26 pigs.

One 130-tonne (128-ton) blue whale weighs about the same as 26 bull African elephants.

Jumbo flying bird

The ostrich is the biggest bird on Earth but, although it can run fast, it is unable to fly. The heaviest bird that can fly is the great bustard, which can weigh as much as the average six-year-old boy – and more than 13,000 times as much as a bee hummingbird.

The average six-year-old boy weighs 20.9 kg (46 lb).

A fully grown great bustard can also weigh 20.9 kg (46 lb).

Lightweight Liberty

Excluding the pedestal, the Statue of Liberty is surprisingly light – only about one-and-a-half times the weight of a fully grown blue whale. It weighs much less than you might expect because, rather than being solid, it is a thin layer of copper over an iron framework.

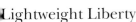

The Statue of Liberty weighs only 204 tonnes (201 tons).

A fully grown blue whale weighs about 130 tonnes (128 tons).

Worth its weight...

Throughout human history, gold has been coveted and valued for its beauty and rarity. Gold is also one of the heaviest of all metals. It is estimated that all the gold ever mined would weigh a total of about 150,000 tonnes (147,638 tons). That sounds like a lot, but in fact it would only make a solid block about the size of a tennis court.

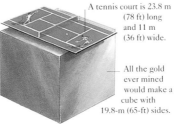

A tennis court is 23.8 m (78 ft) long and 11 m (36 ft) wide.

All the gold ever mined would make a cube with 19.8-m (65-ft) sides.

Big bronze bell

The world's largest bell is the Tsar Kolokol bell at the Kremlin, in Moscow, Russia. Cast from bronze in 1735, it cracked, and has never rung. Amazingly, it is almost as heavy as the much bigger Statue of Liberty.

Excluding the pedestal, the Statue of Liberty is 46 m (151 ft) high and weighs 204 tonnes (201 tons).

The Tsar Kolokol bell is 6.14 m (20 ft) high and weighs 201.9 tonnes (199 tons).

Person drawn to scale

Solid as a rock

Made from more than 2,000,000 blocks of limestone, the Great Pyramid weighs almost 16 times as much as the Empire State Building – which, remarkably, weighs less than the 17-m (56-ft) depth of earth that was excavated for its foundations.

One Empire State Building weighs 331,122 tonnes (325,907 tons) – so 16 of them would weigh 5,297,952 tonnes (5,214,520 tons).

The Great Pyramid weighs an estimated 5,216,400 tonnes (5,134,252 tons).

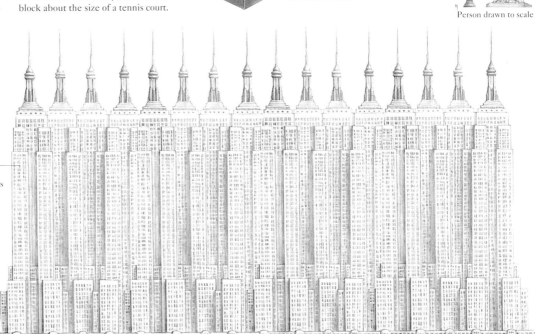

ANIMAL SPEED

SOME ANIMALS ARE CAPABLE of great speed, which they use to chase prey or to escape from predators. Other animals live much more leisurely lives. From the proverbial slowness of the snail to the legendary swiftness of the cheetah – more than 2,000 times as fast – the range of speeds found in the animal world is astonishing. Recording them is not easy, however. Measuring how fast an animal can swim or fly is especially tricky. It is also important not to mistake a sudden spurt for an animal's normal top speed.

Micro movers
The speed of microscopic creatures is expressed in micrometres (millionths of a metre) a second.

Bacteria: up to 100 micrometres a second

Common snail: 0.05 kph (0.03 mph)

Sloth: 0.19 kph (0.12 mph)

Snail's pace
Even at its fastest, the common snail is 100 times slower than a child's normal walking speed.

FLYING THROUGH THE AIR
Birds were the world's fastest creatures until diving World War I aircraft began to exceed even the speed of a diving peregrine falcon, which can touch 350 kph (217 mph). With the aid of wind and gravity, even very small birds can manage 97 kph (60 mph).

Dragonfly: 29 kph (18 mph)

Darting by
Dragonflies are the fastest insects in the world, flying at up to 29 kph (18 mph) – maybe even faster.

As the crow flies
Crows and other common birds average speeds of 32-48 kph (20-30 mph).

Crow: 32-48 kph (20-30 mph)

Guano bat: 51 kph (32 mph)

Batmobility
Active only at night, the speedy guano bat uses sonar to stop it flying into things in the dark.

CHAMPION RUNNERS
Some land animals, such as cheetahs, are sprinters, capable of sudden but short bursts of speed. Others, like elephants, are slower, but can maintain a steady pace for longer.

If cheetahs had to go to school every day, I bet they would be even slower than me!

Heavy going
Despite its great bulk, a charging African elephant can hit 40 kph (25 mph), easily outrunning a human athlete.

African elephant: 40 kph (25 mph)

First steps
A child's normal walking speed – except on the way to school – is just under 5 kph (3 mph).

Child walking: a little less than 5 kph (3 mph)

Fast track
Humans can run a long way at a steady pace, but can only sprint in short bursts. The men's world 100 m record is just under 10 seconds.

Female sprinter: 34 kph (21 mph)

Male sprinter: 36 kph (22 mph)

Cat: 48 kph (30 mph)

Rocketing ratcatchers
Cats can accelerate to 48 kph (30 mph) – which is bad luck for rats, whose top speed is less than 10 kph (6 mph).

SWIM KINGS RULE THE WAVES
The fastest fish and mammals in the sea are generally those with long bodies and powerful tails. Although they rarely exceed 10 times their own body length per second, and the endurance of many is limited, some species are awesome performers in the water.

Dolphin: 48 kph (30 mph)

In the swim
Dolphins can swim at 48 kph (30 mph), and maintain this speed over long distances.

Gentoo penguin: 35 kph (22 mph)

Male swimmer: 8 kph (5 mph)

Penguin power
The gentoo penguin of the Antarctic is thought to be the fastest swimming bird in the world.

At full stretch
Compared with many animals, human swimmers are slowcoaches in the water, with 8 kph (5 mph) the apparent limit for a male Olympic freestyle swimmer.

Sea trout: 24 kph (15 mph)

Quick fish
Sea trout can swim five times as fast as a child can walk.

Tiger shark: 53 kph (33 mph)

Go-faster shark
Tiger sharks can swim six times faster than the fastest humans.

Slow but sure

In the fable, the tortoise won the race against the hare. In real life, the tortoise is one of the slowest animals on land.

SLOWCOACHES OF THE ANIMAL WORLD

Some animals are genuine slowcoaches, but others are handicapped by their tiny size. The top speed of about 5 kph (3 mph) of some cockroaches, for example, is actually a scorching 50 body lengths a second. If a racehorse could do this, it would be able to run at about 490 kph (304 mph) – three times the top speed of a family car.

Slothful progress

Non-stop, it would take a sloth 24 years to stroll around the equator. As sloths sleep for up to 20 hours a day, however, the journey would actually take closer to 144 years.

A flurry of little legs

Large spiders in a hurry can scamper along at 1.8 kph (1.1 mph), but only for a few seconds.

Slow bird

The American woodcock is a real dawdler, flying just fast enough to stay in the air.

Spider:
1.8 kph
(1.1 mph)

Tortoise:
0.37 kph
(0.23 mph)

American woodcock:
8 kph (5 mph)

Harpy eagle:
60-80 kph
(37-50 mph)

Flight of fancy

Although higher speeds are often claimed by pigeon fanciers for their champion racing pigeons, it is unlikely that these birds can exceed 85 kph (53 mph). They are highly prized for their staying power over long distances, however.

Racing pigeon:
85 kph (53 mph)

Duck speed

Ducks are among the fastest birds in level flight, the mallard achieving a top recorded speed of 105 kph (65 mph).

Mallard duck:
105 kph (65 mph)

Swoop to kill

Birds of prey are at their fastest when diving. The fierce harpy eagle uses its speed to swoop down and pluck monkeys and sloths from the branches of trees.

So fast, it's off the page...

The world's fastest bird – in level flight – is almost twice as fast as any shown here. You'll have to turn to page 42 to find out what it is...

Born to run

The fastest thoroughbred racehorses can gallop at nearly 70 kph (43 mph) over short distances – faster still without jockeys on their backs.

Who needs wings?

Although they are too heavy to fly, adult ostriches can outrun racehorses. Quite small chicks can reach 48 kph (30 mph). In South Africa, ostriches are even raced with jockeys on their backs.

On the hoof

Over short distances the pronghorn antelope of North America can run more than twice as fast as a charging African elephant.

On your marks, get set – gone!

The fastest of all land animals, the cheetah, can run at up to 100 kph (62 mph) over short distances. Its amazing acceleration is aided by claws that grip like the spikes of running shoes. If humans ran this fast, the world 100 m record would be a breathtaking 3.6 seconds.

Ostrich:
72 kph
(45 mph)

Pronghorn
antelope:
88 kph
(55 mph)

Cheetah:
100 kph (62 mph)

Racehorse:
70 kph (43 mph)

Out of the blue

Speeds of more than 100 kph (62 mph) have been claimed by some people for the American bluefin tuna, but more reliable scientific tests suggest that 74 kph (46 mph) is its top speed.

The fastest fish in the sea

The sailfish is the undisputed ocean sprint champion, with a recorded peak of 110 kph (68 mph) over short distances. At this speed it could dash the 50-m (164-ft) length of an Olympic swimming pool in only 1.6 seconds – 13 times faster than the quickest human.

Bluefin tuna:
74 kph (46 mph)

Sailfish:
110 kph
(68 mph)

Screaming reels

A favourite catch of deep-sea anglers, the speedy marlin can strip 100 m (328 ft) of line from a fishing reel in less than five seconds.

Marlin:
80 kph
(50 mph)

70 kph (43 mph)   75 kph (47 mph)   80 kph (50 mph)   90 kph (56 mph)   100 kph (62 mph)   110 kph (68 mph)

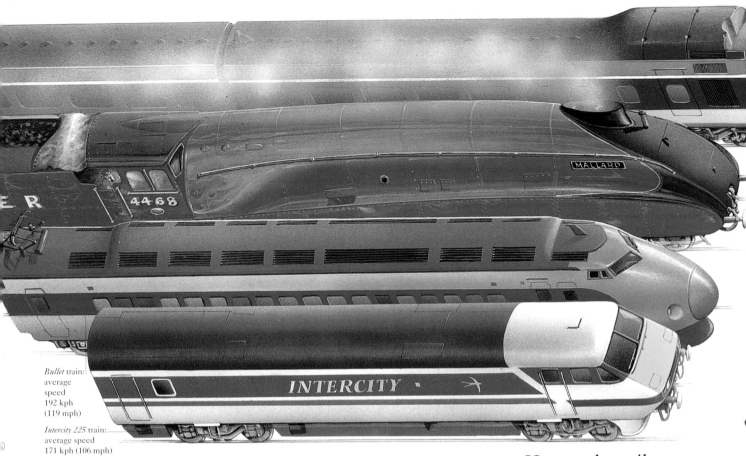

Bullet train: average speed 192 kph (119 mph)

Intercity 225 train: average speed 171 kph (106 mph)

Hot on the rails

The *Intercity 225* is Britain's fastest scheduled passenger train, averaging 171 kph (106 mph).

Le Jamais Contente car: 106 kph (66 mph)

Never satisfied...

Le Jamais Contente (The Never Satisfied), a torpedo-shaped electric car driven by Camille Jenatzy, broke the world land speed record three times, at Achères, in Paris, on 29 April 1899.

Pedal power

The top speed a cyclist has reached without assistance is 89 kph (55 mph), although slipstreaming behind another vehicle to reduce wind resistance has doubled this figure.

Racing cycle: 89 kph (55 mph)

Skateboard: 89 kph (55 mph)

Standing fast

The maximum speed reached by a standing skateboarder is 89 kph (55 mph). Even greater speeds have been recorded when the rider lies down on the board to reduce wind resistance.

Formula One car: 235 kph (146 mph)

On the road

In the 1920s, when cars were first mass-produced, a Model T Ford had a top speed of about 73 kph (45 mph). Today, most standard family cars are capable of more than twice this speed.

Family car: top speed 161 kph (100 mph)

Gone with the wind

The fastest sail-powered craft is not a yacht but a sailboard. Thierry Bielak of France set the world sail speed record on a sailboard in 1991.

The wind is so strong that I'm travelling 10 times faster than an Olympic swimmer.

Sailboard: 83 kph (52 mph)

Catch me if you can, but these boats are so fast I can cover 4 km (2.5 miles) in just one minute.

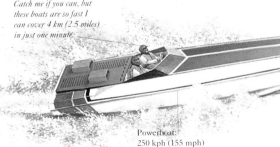

Powerboat: 250 kph (155 mph)

Nuclear submarine: 83 kph (52 mph)

Submarine speed a secret

The top speed of Russian *Alfa*-class nuclear submarines remains a closely guarded military secret, but it is believed that they are capable of up to 83 kph (52 mph). Humans are still quite a bit slower underwater than animals, however. The speedy sailfish is 27 kph (17 mph) faster than this submarine.

LAND AND WATER SPEED

HUMANS ARE FAST MOVERS on land and water – with a little help from a few mechanical friends. Unaided, we are real slowcoaches, and many animals can run and swim much faster. But we have always yearned to go faster and faster, and by using anything from horses to steam engines, from wind power to rockets, we have dramatically increased our speed on land and water. Recently, the all-important sound barrier was broken on land by British driver Andy Green in his vehicle *Thrust SSC*. Such is our urge for speed that eventually all the current records will undoubtedly be broken by machines not even invented yet.

Making tracks

On 3 July 1938 the British locomotive *Mallard* became the fastest steam train of all time. Pulling seven coaches, it reached 203 kph (126 mph) – more than four times the speed of Stevenson's *Rocket*.

Mallard steam train: 203 kph (126 mph)

LAND SPEEDS

Human speed on land was once restricted to running, riding, or using aids such as sledges and skis. But after the development of the railways, more than 150 years ago, speed quickly increased. For a century, trains set almost all the records. Only in the last 50 years have cars been able to beat them.

Cable-car: 35 kph (22 mph)

As fast as a bullet?

Not exactly... A rifle bullet travels at up to 2,635 kph (1,637 mph) – nearly 14 times the speed of Japan's *Bullet* train. However, it is one of the world's fastest railway services, with an average speed of 192 kph (119 mph), and a top speed of 230 kph (143 mph).

Champion cable-car

Travelling between Merida City and the top of Pico Espejo, in Venezuela, the *Teleférico Mérida* is the world's highest, longest, and fastest cable-car.

Rocket power

George Stevenson's *Rocket* was one of the earliest steam locomotives. With a top speed of 47 kph (29 mph), it was faster than any horse-drawn vehicle.

On the run

Top male athletes can sprint at up to 36 kph (22 mph), but are unable to run as fast over long distances.

Rocket steam train: 47 kph (29 mph)

Slowcoach

Horse-drawn stagecoaches were once a common form of transport in many parts of the world. Due to poor roads, their top speed was only 34 kph (21 mph).

LIVERPOOL — MANCHESTER

Olympic runner: 36 kph (22 mph)

Stagecoach: 34 kph (21 mph)

WATER SPEEDS

Humans are slow swimmers – even an Olympic swimmer can reach only about 8 kph (5 mph). Thanks to the invention of powerboats and hydroplanes, however, we can now travel on water at nearly half the speed of sound.

Sailing out in front

Racing yachts can achieve average speeds of more than 18 kph (11 mph), although speeds of double this have been claimed for 19th-century sailing clippers. But the sail speed record was set in Canada in 1990 by the yacht *Longshot*, which reached nearly 69 kph (43 mph).

Longshot yacht: 69 kph (43 mph)

All pulling together

Crews in the UK's annual Oxford and Cambridge boat race row at an average speed of about 24 kph (15 mph) – three times the top speed of a human swimmer.

Dashing dolphins

Swimming in the wakes of ships, speedy dolphins can reach up to 59 kph (37 mph). Without this slipstream effect, their top speed is about 48 kph (30 mph).

Dolphin: 48 kph (30 mph)

Rowing eight: 24 kph (15 mph)

5 kph (3 mph) 10 kph (6 mph) 15 kph (9 mph) 20 kph (12 mph) 30 kph (19 mph) 40 kph (25 mph) 50 kph (31 mph) 60 kph (37 mph)

FASTER AND FASTER

RACING A POWERBOAT, driving a fast car, flying a jet – all provide a thrilling dose of speed. In the excitement it is easy to forget that speed is a modern experience. Our ancestors went no faster than they could ride on horseback. For most people the first taste of speed came with the railways. Flight brought even greater speeds, but not right away. When humans first flew, in 1903, the fastest train could do 210 kph (130 mph), a speed that aircraft did not reach for another 15 years. Space flight is the ultimate thrill. Plummeting back to Earth, the *Apollo 10* astronauts travelled as far in three seconds as they could run in three hours. Space travel is not yet available to all, but long-distance travel on Earth, by land, sea, or air, is now commonplace.

Speedy sky-divers

In August 1960 Joseph Kittinger stepped out of a balloon 31,330 m (102,789 ft) above Tularosa, in New Mexico, in the USA.

Before pulling their rip-cords, sport parachutists relish a few moments of breathtaking speed in free-fall. They accelerate until air resistance stops them from falling faster. Depending on their size, clothing, and posture, they can reach about 195 kph (121 mph). However, plunging from a balloon at 31,330 m (102,789 ft), in 1960, Captain Joseph Kittinger accelerated through the thin air of the upper atmosphere to close to the speed of sound.

In four minutes and 38 seconds, Joseph Kittinger fell 25,820 m (84,711 ft) before his parachute opened – a drop equal to almost 68 Empire State Buildings, or three Mt Everests.

Empire State Building: 381 m (1,250 ft)

Mt Everest: 8,848 m (29,028 ft)

Hopping into the history books

The first powered flight was made in the USA, in 1903, by Orville Wright, and lasted an estimated 12 seconds. We will never know exactly how long Orville was airborne, because his brother Wilbur was so excited that he forgot to stop his stop-watch. The brothers did measure the distance of the flight – at 37 m (120 ft), it was less than the wingspan of a jumbo jet.

The wingspan of a Boeing 747 jumbo jet is 59.6 m (195.5 ft).

On its first flight, the Wright brothers' plane *Flyer* covered only 37 m (120 ft).

Hurrying into the history books

In 1978 Kenneth Warby broke the water speed record on Blowering Dam Lake in his hydroplane *Spirit of Australia*. The specially built powerboat went fast enough to cover the length of the world's longest river in about 13 hours.

At a top speed of 514 kph (319 mph), *Spirit of Australia* went fast enough to cover the 6,670 km (4,145 miles) of the Nile River in about 13 hours.

Fish left far behind

Measuring the speed of fish is not easy, mainly because no-one has yet organized a successful fish race. The gold medal would probably go to the sailfish, which can swim 100 m (328 ft) in little more than three seconds. In a race against *Spirit of Australia*, however, the sailfish would be left trailing.

0   100 kph (62 mph)   200 kph (124 mph)   300 kph (186 mph)   400 kph (249 mph)   500 kph (311 mph)

Sailfish: 110 kph (68 mph)

Spirit of Australia: 514 kph (319 mph)

Marathon journeys by sea and air

Tales of long journeys have always had the power to fascinate. Legend has it that, some 2,500 years ago, an unknown messenger ran 36 km (22.5 miles) non-stop to Athens to bring news of a Greek victory on the battlefield at Marathon – a feat commemorated by the road race of the same name in the Olympic Games. Modern long-distance voyagers set themselves the ultimate challenge: to sail or fly around the world non-stop.

Hi there! By the time we land in Cape Town we will have flown nearly half a million times further than Orville Wright on his historic first flight!

In Germany, in 1972, Hans-Werner Grosse flew a glider non-stop for a record 1,461 km (908 miles).

In 1967 two Sikorsky HH-3E helicopters flew non-stop from New York to Paris, covering a record 6,874 km (4,271 miles). They took 30 hours and 46 minutes to complete the journey at an average speed of 223.5 kph (139 mph).

New York

Paris

In 1981 a helium-filled balloon called *Double Eagle V* flew non-stop from Nagashima, in Japan, to California, covering 8,383 km (5,209 miles). In 1999, the *Breitling Orbiter* completed a record first round-the-world balloon flight, having flown 42,810 km (26,600 miles) in under 20 days.

A Boeing 747 jumbo jet flew non-stop from Paine Field, Washington, USA, to Cape Town, in South Africa, in 1976, covering a record distance for a passenger flight of 16,560 km (10,290 miles).

On the far side of the Moon

In 1970, the crew of *Apollo 13* travelled the furthest anyone has ever travelled from Earth – 400,187 km (248,671 miles), which is more than 31 times the diameter of the planet. An explosion stopped *Apollo 13* from landing on the Moon. Instead, it had to return to Earth by swinging right around the Moon.

The diameter of the Earth is 12,756 km (7,926 miles).

At its furthest, *Apollo 13* was more than 31 times as far away as the diameter of the Earth.

Jumbo jet-lag

At best, a five-hour stagecoach journey in the 18th century might cover a bumpy 60 km (37 miles). Now, allowing for refuelling, Concorde could fly you from London to Singapore in five hours. By jumbo, it actually takes more than twice as long, and while the flight might be smooth, you suffer jet-lag – tiredness caused by flying between very different time zones – for days afterwards.

In five hours, cruising at 2,179 kph (1,354 mph), Concorde could fly the 10,852 km (6,743 miles) between London and Singapore – about the same time it took an 18th-century stagecoach to cover 60 km (37 miles). If Concorde took off at 13:00 in London, therefore, it would be about 18:00 in London when it landed – in Singapore, however, it would be about 02:30 in the morning.

In five hours a Lamborghini *Diablo* – at 325 kph (202 mph) one of the world's fastest road cars – could cover the 1,531 km (951 miles) from Copenhagen, Denmark, to Rome.

In five hours a French *TGV* high-speed train – top speed 515 kph (320 mph) – could cover the 2,486 km (1,545 miles) between Paris and Moscow.

Rome   Copenhagen
0   1,000 km (621 miles)

Paris   Moscow
0   1,000 km   2,000 km (1,243 miles)
(621 miles)

London
0   1,000 km (621 miles)   3,000 km (1,864 miles)   5,000 km (3,107 miles)   7,000 km (4,350 miles)   9,000 km (5,592 miles)

Singapore

Making tracks

In 1891 the Russian tsar began to build a railway line crossing his vast empire. Track was laid from both ends – west from Nakhodka, on the Sea of Japan, and east from Moscow. The world's longest continuous railway line, it goes nearly a quarter of the way around the globe.

The Earth's equator measures 40,075 km (24,902 miles). Totalling 9,438 km (5,865 miles), the Trans-Siberian Railway stretches almost a quarter of the way around the world. It was finished in 1916, just one year before the Russian Revolution toppled the tsar.

The Trans-Siberian Railway is longer than the shortest distance between Paris and Los Angeles – 9,085 km (5,645 miles).

Paris   Los Angeles
0   2,000 km   4,000 km   6,000 km   8,000 km
(1,243 miles)   (2,486 miles)   (3,728 miles)   (4,971 miles)

Supersonic flyers

"Supersonic" means faster than sound. Sound travels more slowly through the cool, thin air of the upper atmosphere. For aircraft, 1,062 kph (660 mph), or Mach 1, is used as the standard speed of sound at altitude. Mach 2 is twice the speed of sound, and so on.

Sound: Mach 1
Bell X-1 rocket plane: Mach 1
Apollo 10 at re-entry: Mach 37
Lockheed SR71A: Mach 3
X-15A-2: Mach 6

0   1,000 kph   3,000 kph   5,000 kph   7,000 kph   30,000 kph
(621 mph)   (1,864 mph)   (3,107 mph)   (4,350 mph)   (18,642 mph)

Crossing America from coast to coast

American settlers heading west in their wagons in the 1840s and 1850s took about six hazardous months to cross the USA. Now the return journey can be done in air-conditioned comfort and safety in less than five hours by jumbo jet.

At 978 kph (608 mph) a jumbo jet can cover the distance between San Francisco and New York in four hours and 38 minutes.

At 6 kph (3.7 mph) it would take 31 days and nine hours to walk 4,517 km (2,807 miles), the distance between San Francisco and New York.

At 7,297 kph (4,534 mph) the X-15A-2 rocket plane could cover the distance between San Francisco and New York in less than 38 minutes.

San Francisco   50 kph   150 kph   900 kph   5,000 kph   New York
(31 mph)   (93 mph)   (559 mph)   (3,107 mph)

At 34 kph (21 mph) a stagecoach would take five days and 13 hours to travel 4,517 km (2,807 miles).

At 72 kph (45 mph) it would take a 1923 Model T Ford two days and 15 hours to travel 4,517 km (2,807 miles).

At 165 kph (103 mph) the *Empire State Express* could travel the distance from San Francisco to New York in less than 28 hours.

In 1986 a specially built plane, *Voyager*, became the first to fly non-stop around the world without refuelling. It landed back in California nine days, three minutes and 44 seconds after taking off.

GRAF ZEPPELIN

Graf Zeppelin was the first rigid airship to fly all the way around the world, in August 1929. It arrived back in New Jersey 21 days, five hours and 31 minutes after setting out, having flown at least 35,200 km (21,873 miles).

In 1968-69, in his boat *Suhaili*, Robin Knox-Johnson became the first person to sail, single-handedly, non-stop around the world. He covered a total of 48,478 km (30,122 miles) in 312 days.

20,000 km (12,428 miles)   25,000 km (15,535 miles)   30,000 km (18,642 miles)   35,000 km (21,749 miles)

Driverless sled dash

The unofficial land speed record, set by *Budweiser Rocket*, currently stands at 1,190 kph (739 mph), but this is not the fastest that a vehicle has ever travelled on land. In New Mexico in 1959, an unmanned US Air Force rocket sled on rails achieved the incredible speed of 4,972 kph (3,090 mph) – four times the speed of sound.

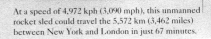

Budweiser Rocket reached 1,190 kph (739 mph) – less than a quarter the speed of the fastest unmanned vehicle on Earth.

At a speed of 4,972 kph (3,090 mph), this unmanned rocket sled could travel the 5,572 km (3,462 miles) between New York and London in just 67 minutes.

Special achievement

In 1947, British speed ace John Cobb, driving the streamlined *Railton Mobil Special*, set a new land speed record that stood for more than 15 years. He reached 634 kph (394 mph) – more than half the speed of sound.

Swift by name, swift by nature

Imagine that you are speeding along in a train. You look out of the window and see a bird flying alongside. Nothing unusual in that – but you might be surprised if you looked again a few minutes later and the bird was still there. It is not impossible – the aptly named spine-tailed swift can fly as fast as a British *Intercity 225*.

Both the spine-tailed swift and the *Intercity 225* can reach a speed of 171 kph (106 mph).

Into the jet age

In 1964, jet-powered cars took over from wheel-driven cars in the chase for the world land speed record. In 1965, Craig Breedlove of the USA became the first person to top 967 kph (600 mph), in his car *Spirit of America – Sonic 1*.

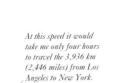

At this speed it would take me only four hours to travel the 3,936 km (2,446 miles) from Los Angeles to New York.

THE BLUE FLAME

Blue Flame car: 1,002 kph (622 mph)

Faster than a jumbo jet

American racer Gary Gabelich broke the world land speed record in his rocket-engined car, *Blue Flame*, on 23 October 1970 at Bonneville Salt Flats. His amazing speed of 1,002 kph (622 mph) was faster than a Boeing 747 jumbo jet.

The speed of sound

The fastest man on wheels is British driver Andy Green, who broke the sound barrier by reaching a speed of 1,227.99 kph (763.04 mph) in his car, *Thrust SSC* in the Black Rock Desert, USA, on 15 October 1997. American film stuntman Stan Barrett, who reached 1,190 kph (739 mph) in *Budweiser Rocket* in 1979 at Edwards Air Force Base, had set the previous world record.

Bluebird car: 649 kph (403 mph)

Budweiser Rocket car: 1,190 kph (739 mph)

No contest

The sleepy sloth spends up to 20 hours a day dozing, and when it wakes moves at a truly slothful pace – a maximum speed of 0.19 kph (0.12 mph). The sloth's leisurely progress contrasts with that of the rapid French *TGV* train, which travels more than 1,294 times as fast as the sloth on its scheduled run, and 2,710 times as fast at record speed.

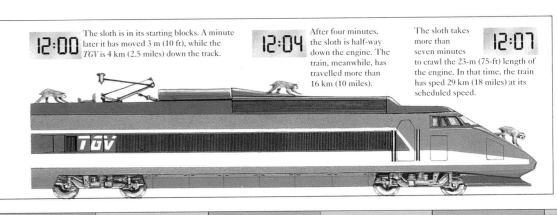

12:00 The sloth is in its starting blocks. A minute later it has moved 3 m (10 ft), while the *TGV* is 4 km (2.5 miles) down the track.

12:04 After four minutes, the sloth is half-way down the engine. The train, meanwhile, has travelled more than 16 km (10 miles).

12:07 The sloth takes more than seven minutes to crawl the 23-m (75-ft) length of the engine. In that time, the train has sped 29 km (18 miles) at its scheduled speed.

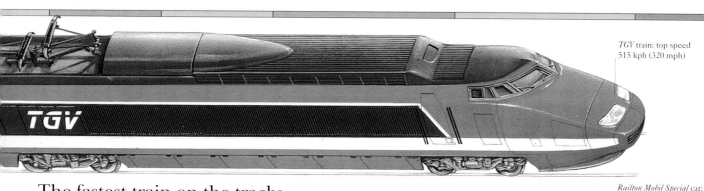

TGV train: top speed
515 kph (320 mph)

The fastest train on the tracks

The French *Train à Grande Vitesse* (TGV), or High Speed Train, set
the world record speed for a locomotive on 18 May 1990 when it
reached 515 kph (320 mph) – more than 10 times the speed of *Rocket*.
Its regular 254.3-kph (158-mph) journey between Massy and St Pierre
is also the fastest scheduled rail service in the world.

Railton Mobil Special car:
634 kph (394 mph)

Bluebird 2 car:
485 kph (301 mph)

Bird tops bike speed

In a steep dive to impress its mate, a male
peregrine falcon can touch 350 kph (217 mph) –
faster than the fastest motorcycle.

Peregrine falcon:
350 kph (217 mph)

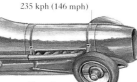

Flat out

In 1935 Malcolm
Campbell set another
of his land speed
records, this time in
Bluebird 2. He reached 485 kph
(301 mph) at Bonneville Salt Flats, Utah, USA.

Bluebird 1 car:
235 kph (146 mph)

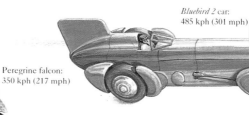

Dragged to a halt

Drag cars travel so fast that they cannot be
stopped by ordinary brakes, and have to use
parachutes to slow them down. These cars race
along a straight, 400-m (0.25-mile) course,
accelerating from a standing start to
three times the top speed
of a family car.

Spirit of America – Sonic 1:
967 kph (600 mph)

SPIRIT OF AMERICA

First of nine

In 1924, Malcolm Campbell took his
Bluebird car up to 235 kph (146 mph), the
first of nine land speed records he was to set.

Wheel-driven drag car:
497 kph (309 mph)

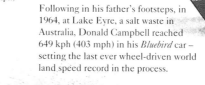

In the fast lane

The fastest Formula One
circuit average of 235 kph
(146 mph) was recorded by
British driver Nigel Mansell
in a Williams-Honda in the
1987 Austrian Grand Prix.

Motorcycle: almost
300 kph (186 mph)

End of an era

Following in his father's footsteps, in
1964, at Lake Eyre, a salt waste in
Australia, Donald Campbell reached
649 kph (403 mph) in his *Bluebird* car –
setting the last ever wheel-driven world
land speed record in the process.

Speedy superbikes

Modern motorcycles are more than three
times as quick as the fastest bicycle.
Japanese "superbikes" can reach top
speeds of almost 300 kph (186 mph).

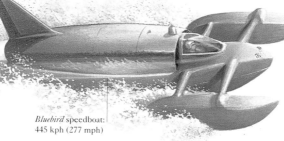

Bird on the water

In 1964, the same year he broke
the world land speed record in his
Bluebird car, Donald Campbell set a
new world water speed record in his
Bluebird speedboat, with a speed of
445 kph (277 mph).

Bluebird speedboat:
445 kph (277 mph)

Spirit of Australia hydroplane:
514 kph (319 mph)

Pacy powerboats

Powerboats certainly live up to their
name, being capable of speeds of more
than 250 kph (155 mph) – at least 10
times as fast as the eight-man rowing
crews in the annual Oxford and
Cambridge boat race.

Spirited skimmer

The official world water speed
record is held by a hydroplane –
a flat-bottomed motor boat that
skims along the surface of the
water. The record was set by
Kenneth Warby on 8 October
1978, in *Spirit of Australia*.

SPEEDO 7

250 kph (155 mph)   275 kph (171 mph)   300 kph (186 mph)   400 kph (249 mph)   500 kph (311 mph)

AIR SPEED

HISTORY WAS MADE one winter morning in 1903, when two American bicycle mechanics towed a fragile timber and cloth aircraft on to a sandy North Carolina beach, started its noisy engine, and flew. The Wright brothers, Wilbur and Orville, were the world's first pilots, but their *Flyer* would have won no prizes for speed. It flew at only 48 kph (30 mph), and on its longest flight it took nearly one minute to cover only 260 m (852 ft). In 1967, only 64 years after the Wright brothers first flew, the X-15A-2 rocket plane flew more than 150 times faster. In the 59 seconds that the *Flyer* was airborne at Kill Devil Hills, Kitty Hawk, the X-15A-2 could have flown past Norfolk, Virginia, some 120 km (75 miles) away.

Speedy Spitfire
At the start of World War II (1939-45), the British Supermarine Spitfire was the world's fastest fighter aircraft. The fastest Spitfire, the Mk XIV, flew four times as fast as the natural world's fastest flyer, the spine-tailed swift.

Wright kite
The Wright brothers chose North Carolina's Outer Banks as the site to test their *Flyer* because the strong, steady winds there helped to lift the aircraft into the air, like a kite.

Westland *Lynx*: 400 kph (249 mph)

Three-winged fighter
Although no faster than the world's fastest bird, the Fokker Dr.I triplane was one of the most successful German fighter aircraft of World War I (1914-18). Flying a red-painted model, Manfred von Richthofen, the famous Red Baron, shot down 80 enemy planes.

Chop chop!
The world's fastest helicopter, the Westland *Lynx*, can fly at up to 400 kph (249 mph) – almost 14 times faster than the world's fastest insects, dragonflies. However, in normal use and fully loaded with 10 troops or two torpedoes, it cruises at about two-thirds of this speed.

Supermarine Spitfire Mk XIV: 721 kph (448 mph)

Flyer: 48 kph (30 mph)

Fokker Dr.I: 165 kph (103 mph)

Dawdling doodlebugs
V1 flying bombs, or doodlebugs, developed by Germany during World War II, were pilotless aircraft laden with explosives. Slower than fighter planes, they could be shot down, and less than half reached their targets.

V1 flying bomb: 563 kph (350 mph)

Stately pioneer
Although slower than the top speed of a modern family car, the *Hindenburg* airship was the world's first transatlantic passenger service by air, crossing between Germany and the USA.

Hindenburg: cruising speed 126 kph (78 mph)

Silent swoopers
Gliders are unpowered aircraft that soar on rising currents of warm air. They can swoop at up to 320 kph (199 mph) – faster than the fastest motorcycle – but cruise at half this speed.

Glider: 320 kph (199 mph)

Swift birds
Spine-tailed swifts can fly faster than any aircraft built before World War I.

Spine-tailed swift: 171 kph (106 mph)

Feathered flight
A skilled archer can fire a longbow arrow fast enough to spear the world's fastest helicopter.

Longbow arrow: 550 kph (342 mph)

Keep pedalling!
Human-powered aircraft have huge wings to lift them into the air at very low speeds. In 1979, Bryan Allen pedalled *Gossamer Albatross* across the English Channel so slowly – half the speed of the Wright brothers' *Flyer* – that it barely cleared the waves.

Gossamer Albatross: 24 kph (15 mph)

Plunging birds
Peregrine falcons can dive as fast as the landing speed of a space shuttle.

Peregrine falcons can dive at 350 kph (217 mph).

Super sea-plane
From 1913-31, competition for the Schneider Trophy for sea-planes repeatedly raised the air speed record. After winning the final contest as the only entrant, the British Supermarine S.6B set a record of 610 kph (379 mph) – faster than a speeding arrow. Two weeks later it broke the 644 kph (400 mph) barrier. It was later modified into the Spitfire fighter.

Touchdown!
The speed of a space shuttle on landing is more than three times as fast as the top speed of the fastest land animal on Earth, the cheetah.

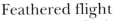

Supermarine S.6B 655 kph (407 mph)

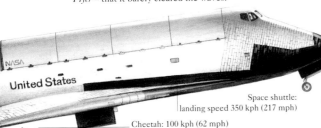

Space shuttle: landing speed 350 kph (217 mph)

Cheetah: 100 kph (62 mph)

Concorde: cruising speed 2,179 kph (1,354 mph)

For people in a hurry...

Concorde is the world's fastest passenger aircraft. Holding up to 130 passengers, it can fly from New York to London in under three hours. The same journey takes more than twice as long in an ordinary passenger aircraft.

Hi, down there! At this speed you could cross the Atlantic eight times in one day – although after the first few times you wouldn't know if you were coming or going!

Yeager goes supersonic

Until the 1940s, many people believed that it would be impossible to fly faster than the speed of sound – about 1,229 kph (764 mph) near the ground, and 1,062 kph (660 mph) in the thinner upper atmosphere. Then, in 1947, American pilot Charles Yeager broke the sound barrier – Mach 1 – in a specially built, rocket-powered aircraft, the Bell X-1. Like the later X-15A and X-15A-2, the Bell X-1 was launched high in the air from a bomber.

Bell X-1: 1,128 kph (701 mph)

X-15A-2 tops the lot

The fastest aircraft of all time, the 1960s North American X-15A-2, did not take off from a runway in the conventional way. Instead, a B-52 bomber ferried it to its cruising altitude, where its rocket engines blasted it to a maximum speed more than 150 times as fast as the Wright brothers' *Flyer*.

X-15A-2: maximum speed 7,297 kph (4,534 mph)

V2 rocket: 5,700 kph (3,542 mph)

Rocket bombs

Pioneering German rocket engineers built 3,610 V2 missiles towards the end of World War II. Aimed at cities, V2s travelled more than twice as fast as an ordinary rifle bullet.

Lockheed SR71A: 3,530 kph (2,193 mph)

Blackbird scorches speed record

The world air speed record for an aircraft taking off from the ground was set by the US Air Force in a Lockheed SR71A spy plane, in 1976. Nicknamed *Blackbird*, it flew more than 70 times as fast as the Wright brothers' *Flyer*.

Boeing 747: cruising speed 978 kph (608 mph)

Cruising the skies

Boeing 747 jumbo jet passenger planes cruise at close to the speed of sound, and more than seven times as fast as the *Hindenburg* airship.

Up, up and away!

Aviators aiming for record heights quickly run out of air. Balloonists need it to buoy up their gas-filled envelopes. Pilots control aircraft using the flow of air over rudder, ailerons, and elevators, but the record breaking X-15A also used tiny rockets for extra control in the thin air of the upper atmosphere.

In August 1963, American test pilot Joseph Walker flew his X-15A over Edwards Air Force Base to 107,960 m (354,200 ft) – more than 12 times the height of Mt Everest.

In May 1961, Malcolm Ross and Victor Prather rose in a gas balloon from the deck of the USS *Antietam* to 34,668 m (113,740 ft) above the Gulf of Mexico – almost four times the height of Mt Everest.

Foxbat flies flat-out

Although designed back in the 1960s, the Russian MiG-25 is still the world's fastest combat aircraft. Nicknamed *Foxbat*, it can fly almost 10 times as fast as a diving peregrine falcon.

MiG-25: 3,395 kph (2,110 mph)

Fighter folds its wings

The main European combat aircraft, the Panavia *Tornado*, has wings that fold back during supersonic flight, much like the wings of a swooping spine-tailed swift. The *Tornado* is almost 14 times faster, however.

Tornado: 2,357 kph (1,465 mph)

Jet jumps into the air

By pointing the jet nozzles of the BAe *Harrier* downwards, the pilot can take off vertically, just like a bird. Swivelled to the horizontal position, the nozzles thrust the fighter plane forward to more than the speed of sound.

BAe *Harrier*: 1,190 kph (739 mph)

Shooting ahead

An ordinary rifle bullet flies fast enough to put a hole in all but the world's fastest fighter aircraft.

Back to the drawing board...

Power for the tiny Messerschmitt 163 *Komet* came from a single rocket, which accelerated it to almost twice the speed of an arrow. The plane had little impact on World War II, however, because it was uncontrollable at top speed, and ran out of fuel after only 10 minutes.

Me 163 *Komet*: 1,004 kph (624 mph)

Rifle bullet: 2,635 kph (1,637 mph)

Mt Everest: 8,848 m (29,028 ft)

kph (435 mph) | 800 kph (497 mph) | 900 kph (559 mph) | 1,000 kph (621 mph) | 3,000 kph (1,864 mph) | 5,000 kph (3,107 mph) | 7,000 kph (4,350 mph)

GREAT CAPACITIES

IT IS EASIER TO GRASP the widths, heights, and lengths of things such as giant supertankers and sports stadiums than it is to imagine their volumes and capacities – the amount of space they contain, and how much of something it takes to fill that space. The reason is simple: when the width, height, and length of something doubles, its volume increases eightfold, not twofold. This rule explains the almost unbelievable fact that the fleet of lorries required to deliver enough standard containers to fill the huge Vehicle Assembly Building at the Kennedy Space Center would stretch as far as from Paris to Rome. It also explains the equally amazing fact that just one tower can hold enough water for someone to have a bath every day of the year for 65 years.

In case of another oil shortage...

Saudi Arabia is the world's largest oil producer, so it is not surprising that it also has the world's largest oil storage facilities. Each of the five colossal oil tanks at Ju'aymah is taller than a four-storey town house, and wider than the length of a soccer pitch. Each can hold 307,500,000 litres (67,641,882 gallons), or 1,500,000 barrels, of oil. If the oil were petroleum, each tank could hold enough for the average car to drive to the Moon and back about 6,000 times.

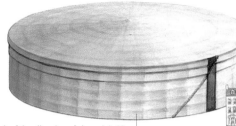

Each of the oil tanks at Ju'aymah is 22 m (72 ft) high and 118 m (387 ft) wide.

Four-storey town house: 20 m (66 ft) tall

One very big refinery

The largest oil refinery in the world is in Judibana, Falcón, Venezuela. The *Petroleos de Venezuela* can process 108,650,000 litres (23,900,131 gallons), or 530,000 barrels, of crude oil a day – one barrel being 205 litres (45 gallons). In one year, this is equivalent to refining all the oil in 61 large supertankers, each holding about 650,000,000 litres (142,982,840 gallons), or about 3,170,000 barrels – more than one supertanker a week.

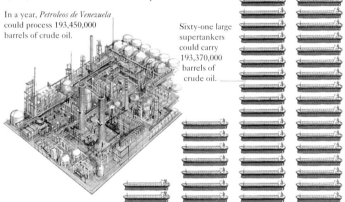

In a year, *Petroleos de Venezuela* could process 193,450,000 barrels of crude oil.

Sixty-one large supertankers could carry 193,370,000 barrels of crude oil.

Supertankers swallow storage tanks

Even bigger than the largest container ships, the largest supertankers in the world can hold about 650,000,000 litres (142,982,840 gallons), or about 3,170,000 barrels, of oil – more than twice as much as one of the five giant storage tanks at Ju'aymah, in Saudi Arabia.

Two Ju'aymah tanks: 3,000,000 barrels of oil

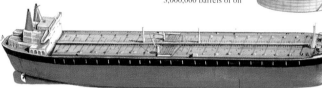

Supertankers can be 485 m (1,591 ft) long and 70 m (230 ft) wide, and can carry 3,170,000 barrels of oil.

Four-storey town house: 20 m (66 ft) tall

Dresden Express, one of the world's largest container ships, is 294 m (965 ft) long and 40 m (131 ft) wide.

Space centre has lorryloads of room

Built in 1965 for the huge *Saturn V* rockets, the Vehicle Assembly Building at the Kennedy Space Center, Florida, USA, is one of the largest buildings in the world. It is 218 m (715 ft) long and 158 m (518 ft) wide, with one bay 160 m (525 ft) high, and another bay 64 m (210 ft) high. Its total volume is 3,664,993 cubic m (129,427,300 cubic ft) – room enough to stack about 100,000 standard containers. Were all the containers to be delivered on the same day, the queue of lorries would stretch about as far as from Paris to Rome.

Bath time – again

The waterspheroid water tower in Edmond, Oklahoma, in the USA, holds 1,893,000 litres (416,410 gallons) when full. Allowing 80 litres (17.5 gallons) for a bath, that is enough water for 23,663 baths – one every day of the year for 65 years.

Edmond waterspheroid: 49 m (161 ft) tall

Each tub represents about 500 baths

Hi! Only 23,662 more to go... I wonder if I've got enough soap?

The Edmond waterspheroid can hold enough water for 23,663 baths.

Four-storey town house: 20 m (66 ft)

Carrying containers by the thousand

Bulk products such as coal and wheat are carried loose in dry-cargo ships, but valuable goods such as clothes and electronic equipment are carried in container ships. Sealed metal containers allow all sorts of goods to be carried, without damage by sea. Refrigerated containers allow even perishable goods, such as meat, to be carried all around the world. The more containers a ship can carry, the cheaper it is to move each container. Built in 1991, *Dresden Express*, one of the largest container ships in the world, has an overall capacity of 4,422 standard containers.

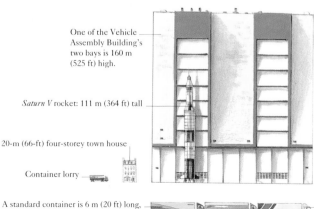

One of the Vehicle Assembly Building's two bays is 160 m (525 ft) high.

Saturn V rocket: 111 m (364 ft) tall

20-m (66-ft) four-storey town house

Container lorry

A standard container is 6 m (20 ft) long, 2.4 m (8 ft) high, and 2.4 m (8 ft) wide, and is about 36 cubic m (1,280 cubic ft).

Paris

Dresden Express

Container lorry

Allowing slightly more than 10 m (33 ft) for each lorry, 100,000 standard container lorries would stretch about as far as the 1,105 km (687 miles) from Paris to Rome.

Rome

Built in the 1930s, *Graf Zeppelin II* was 245 m (804 ft) long, and held almost 200,000 cubic m (7,062,895 cubic ft) of hydrogen. (Her sister airship, *Hindenburg*, was just as big.)

Gigantic gasholder

The world's largest gasholder, at Simmering, Vienna, Austria, is as tall as the largest living thing on Earth, the General Sherman giant sequoia. When full, it holds enough gas to fill either of the two largest airships ever built one-and-a-half times over. The same amount of gas could also fill four of the biggest-ever hot-air balloons, or 138 ordinary hot-air balloons.

Four-storey town house: 20 m (66 ft) tall

The General Sherman giant sequoia, in California, USA, is 84 m (276 ft) tall.

The Simmering gasholder is 84 m (276 ft) tall and holds 300,000 cubic m (10,594,342 cubic ft) of gas when full.

One of the largest hot-air balloons ever flown, the *Virgin Otsuka Pacific Flyer*, held 73,624 cubic m (2,600,000 cubic ft) of hot air. Richard Branson and Per Lindstrand flew it across the Pacific Ocean in 1991.

A standard hot-air balloon holds 2,180 cubic m (76,986 cubic ft) of hot air.

By the coachload

The capacities of single-decker buses and coaches vary around the world, but 49 passengers is about the average.

The average single-decker coach can hold 49 passengers.

By the jetload

The number of passenger seats that a Boeing 747 jumbo jet contains varies from airline to airline, and depends on the type of seats, how the seats are arranged, and the amount of room allowed for each passenger. The maximum number, however, is 570 – almost 12 coachloads.

The maximum passenger capacity of a jumbo jet is 570.

Almost 12 coachloads of people are needed to fill a jumbo jet, at its maximum capacity.

By the boatload

In addition to 350 cars and 60 lorries, the *Silja Europa* ferry, which operates between Finland and Sweden, can carry up to 3,000 passengers – more than five times as many as a jumbo jet.

The *Silja Europa* ferry is 30 m (98 ft) wide and 200 m (656 ft) long. It can hold 3,000 passengers.

It would take more than five jumbo jetloads of passengers to fill the *Silja Europa* ferry.

Pulling in the crowds

The *Circus Maximus* arena of ancient Rome is said to have held upwards of 250,000 people. The largest stadium in the modern world, the open Strahov Stadium, in Prague, in the Czech Republic, could hold about 240,000 spectators when it was completed in 1934 – more than twice as many as the world's biggest covered stadiums. It was built to accommodate mass gymnastics displays featuring up to 40,000 people performing in unison. To fill the Strahov Stadium would require 80 full *Silja Europa* ferries... or 421 full jumbo jets... or 4,898 full coaches.

When completed in 1934, the Strahov Stadium could hold 240,000 spectators.

It would take 80 full *Silja Europa* ferries to fill the Strahov Stadium.

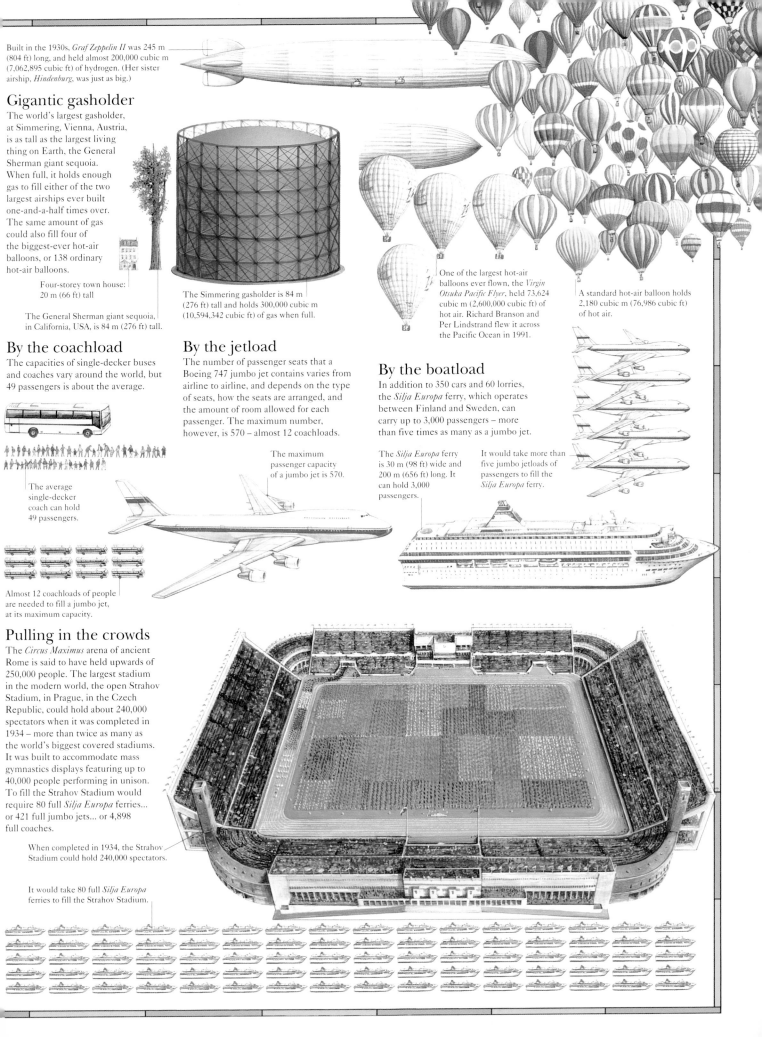

BIG BUILDINGS

THE WORLD'S TALLEST buildings are the twin structures of the 452-m (1,482-ft) Petronas Towers, in Kuala Lumpur, Malaysia, opened in 1996. They overtook the 110-storey Sears Tower in Chicago. Even taller buildings are planned around the world, although work on several in Asia has been suspended for economic reasons. Among these is the Shanghai World Financial Center in Shanghai, China; if completed, its 94 storeys will soar to 460 m (1,509 ft). There are even higher structures, such as television masts. These are so tall and thin that they are not self-supporting – they are held up with strong cables. The tallest structure ever built was a television mast near Warsaw, in Poland. It was a cloud-tickling 646 m (2,119 ft), but fell in 1991 while it was being repaired. As a result, the world's tallest structure is now the KTHI-TV mast in North Dakota, in the USA.

Four-storey town house: 20 m (66 ft)

Head for heights

A four-storey town house is like a doll's house compared with the Statue of Liberty.

Viewing gallery in head

Statue of Liberty: 23 m (75 ft) from shoulders to torch

Packing them in

Modern office buildings are designed to hold many people on large floor areas. If you draw St Peter's, the Empire State Building, and one of the two World Trade Center towers in proportion to how many people each can hold, you get this result.

World Trade Center tower: Completed 1973 Holds 25,000 people

Empire State Building: Completed 1931 Holds 15,000 people

St Peter's: Completed 1590 Holds 3,000 people

The corridors of power

St Peter's church would fit twice into the ground area occupied by the Great Pyramid. But both buildings are dwarfed by the vast floor area of the Pentagon, a US government building in Washington, DC. With its maze of corridors, the five-sided Pentagon is the largest office complex in the world.

Hello there – I'm lost! There are about 27 km (17 miles) of corridors here. That's a minimum four-hour walk. Help!

Pentagon: 117,355 sq m (1,263,240 sq ft)

Great Pyramid: 53,095 sq m (571,530 sq ft)

St Peter's: 36,446 sq m (392,310 sq ft)

Built to last

The Great Pyramid is almost entirely solid, so an immense amount of stone was used to build it – more than 2,500,000 cubic m (88,286,188 cubic ft). The same volume of brick and stone would build 40 Empire State Buildings.

40 Empire State Buildings

1 Great Pyramid

High office

At 243 m (797 ft), 1 Canada Square, at Canary Wharf, in London, is the UK's tallest office building. A chain of 8,000 paper clips dangled from the top floor would just about reach the ground.

1 Canada Square

High church

With its enormous dome, St Peter's, in Rome, Italy, rises to 137.5 m (451 ft) – almost the length of two jumbo jets.

Desert wonder

It would take about 70 camels standing on each other's backs to reach the top of the Great Pyramid, at Giza, in Egypt. Built some 4,500 years ago as the tomb of King Khufu, it is 147 m (481 ft) high.

Missing top stone included in height

Great Pyramid

Twin peaks

Cologne Cathedral, in Germany, has twin spires that are each 156 m (513 ft) high. When built, in the 1880s, they were the world's tallest artificial structures.

Cologne Cathedral

Toppling tower

At 55 m (180 ft), the Leaning Tower of Pisa, in Italy, is nearly three times as high as a four-storey town house.

Four-storey town house: 20 m (66 ft)

Leaning Tower

Lofty statue

The Statue of Liberty, in New York, in the USA, is 93 m (305 ft) high from the base of the pedestal to the torch.

St Peter's

Statue of Liberty

600 m (1,969 ft)

500 m (1,640 ft)

400 m (1,312 ft)

300 m (984 ft)

200 m (656 ft)

100 m (328 ft)

0

Put in their place

Compared with the world's great mountain ranges, such as the lofty Himalayas, even the tallest buildings are really very small indeed. It would take no fewer than 27 Eiffel Towers stacked one on top of the other to reach the peak of Mt Everest, the world's highest mountain. Even the tallest artificial structure in the world, North Dakota's KTHI-TV mast, would fit 14 times into the height of Everest. As for 20-m (66-ft), four-storey town houses, you would need no fewer than 443 of them to reach the top of the world's highest mountain.

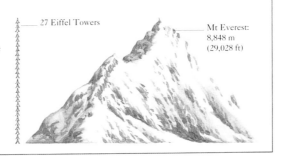

27 Eiffel Towers

Mt Everest:
8,848 m
(29,028 ft)

On a high wire

The KTHI-TV mast, in North Dakota, rises to 629 m (2,063 ft). Supported by guy wires, it is the tallest artificial structure in the world.

KTHI-TV mast

Standing tall

The world's highest self-supporting tower, at 553 m (1,815 ft), is the CN Tower, in Toronto, in Canada. It is five times as tall as the world's tallest tree.

THE ONLY WAY IS UP

Great advances in engineering mean modern buildings can be much taller than those of past centuries. Older buildings have solid, heavy walls, but today's skyscrapers have lightweight outer frameworks of steel and glass. The tallest modern buildings are in city centres. So many people want to live and work in city centres that skyscrapers are the only way to fit everyone in.

High fliers

The World Trade Center, in New York, has two towers, the taller of which rises to 419 m (1,375 ft).

It's official

For many years the world's tallest office building was the Sears Tower, in Chicago, at 443 m (1,453 ft) high – four times as tall as a *Saturn V* rocket.

CN Tower

Sears Tower

World Trade Center

Celebrity 'scraper

The world's best-known skyscraper is the 102-storey Empire State Building, in New York. It is 381 m (1,250 ft) tall, not counting the mast. Like other skyscrapers, it has warning beacons for low-flying aircraft.

Empire State Building

Towering success

At 321 m (1,052 ft) tall – including the radio mast – the Eiffel Tower, in Paris, France, is 16 times as tall as a 20-m (66-ft), four-storey town house. It was built for the 1889 Paris Exhibition, and remains a popular tourist attraction.

High finance

It would take a stack of 8,268 standard size (3.81-cm/1.5-in high) gold bars to reach the top of the 315-m (1,033-ft) tall Bank of China Building, in Hong Kong.

Corporate structure

The Chrysler Building, in New York, is 319 m (1,046 ft) high to the top of its spire – equivalent to 60 of the city's famous yellow taxicabs stuck bumper to bumper in a traffic jam.

Chrysler Building

Bank of China Building

Eiffel Tower

I'm on the tower's second level. Only 952 more steps to the top – I think I'll take the lift!

Four-storey town house

Saturn V rocket: 111m (364 ft)

600 m (1,969 ft)

500 m (1,640 ft)

400 m (1,312 ft)

300 m (984 ft)

200 m (656 ft)

100 m (328 ft)

0

HUMAN POPULATION

A POPULATION EXPLOSION has seen the number of people in the world more than triple since 1900 – from less than 2,000,000,000 – to more than 6,000,000,000 at the end of the 20th century. Each day, enough people to fill the largest stadium in the world are added to the total. Thankfully, the world is a very big place. All the people in the world today could actually fit, standing shoulder to shoulder, on the small Indonesian island of Bali. Most of the world is only sparsely inhabited, and there are more people in some cities than there are in some of the largest countries. But nowhere do you find more people than in China – 20 per cent of all the people in the world live in this huge country.

Of the 6,000,000,000 or so people in the world, about 1,256,000,000 live in China. This means that, worldwide, almost one person in five lives in China.

China grows and grows

China's population is bigger than that of any other country. Government policies now restrict couples in China from having more than one child, but even so it is predicted that the country's population will reach 1,477,730,000 by the year 2050.

There are more people in China today than there were in the whole world as recently as 150 years ago.

China, the USA, and Australia mapped in proportion to their populations

Only about 18,500,000 people live in Australia, mainly in coastal cities. Large areas of this vast country are desert.

The population of the USA (including Alaska and Hawaii) is about 274,000,000 – 15 times bigger than that of Australia.

China's population of 1,256,000,000 is five times bigger than that of the USA, and 67 times bigger than that of Australia.

China's population in perspective

China covers an area only slightly greater than that of the USA, while Australia is not far behind China and the USA as one of the world's largest countries. However, the population of China is nearly five times greater than that of the USA, and an amazing 67 times greater than that of Australia. When the maps of these three countries are redrawn to a scale in proportion to their populations, rather than their actual areas, you can see just how vast the population of China really is.

Australia is the fifth largest country in the world – after Russia, Canada, China, and the USA – but has a population no bigger than that of Sri Lanka.

Land and people...

Japan and Zimbabwe are countries with almost exactly the same land areas, but with very different populations. In terms of population, it would take 11.5 Zimbabwes to equal one Japan.

The population of Japan is about 126,000,000.

The population of Zimbabwe is about 11,000,000.

People and land...

Australia and Sri Lanka are countries with similar populations, but Sri Lanka would fit into Australia 119 times. If Australia were as densely populated as Sri Lanka, Australia's population would be more than 2,000,000,000. If Sri Lanka were as sparsely populated as Australia, Sri Lanka's population would be only about 150,000.

The population of Sri Lanka is about 18,000,000.

Size by area

In this box, all the countries featured on these two pages are drawn in proportion to their actual size, in area.

China: 9,596,960 sq km (3,705,676 sq miles)

USA: 9,529,063 sq km (3,679,459 sq miles)

Australia: 7,836,848 sq km (3,026,044 sq miles)

Sudan: 2,505,813 sq km (967,570 sq miles)

Zimbabwe: 390,580 sq km (150,815 sq miles)

Japan: 377,800 sq km (145,880 sq miles)

South Korea: 99,020 sq km (38,235 sq miles)

Sri Lanka: 65,610 sq km (25,334 sq miles)

Bali: 5,620 sq km (2,170 sq miles)

Population pyramids

Living standards in a country are reflected in the age structure of its population. In poor countries, families tend to be large, but few people survive to old age. In rich countries, by contrast, families tend to be small, and better living conditions mean that many more people survive to old age. The difference is clear if you look at the age structures of Rwanda, a poor country, and Sweden, a rich one, as "population pyramids". These two countries have similar total populations, but very different numbers of young and old people.

Age 75+: 50,000 (0.6%)

Age 60-74: 270,000 (3.4%)

Age 45-59: 591,000 (7.5%)

Age 30-44: 1,095,000 (14%)

Age 15-29: 2,150,000 (27.5%)

Age 0-14: 3,651,000 (47%)

RWANDA
(population 7,807,000)

Age 75+: 715,000 (8%)

Age 60-74: 1,223,000 (14%)

Age 45-59: 1,685,000 (19%)

Age 30-44: 1,790,000 (20.5%)

Age 15-29: 1,720,000 (19.5%)

Age 0-14: 1,652,000 (19%)

SWEDEN
(population 8,785,000)

Crowding the court

All cities are crowded, but some are more crowded than others. Take the population densities of London and Hong Kong Island. Hong Kong Island is so closely packed that if it were divided into tennis courts there would be 25 people on each court. In London there would be only one person on each court.

Hong Kong Island: 25 people in an area the size of a tennis court

A tennis court covers 261 sq m (2,808 sq ft).

London: one person in an area the size of a tennis court

Colossal conurbation

When two or more cities grow until they merge, they form a conurbation. The population of the conurbation of Tokyo and Yokahama, in Japan, is about as big as the population of Sudan, a large country that is mainly uninhabited desert.

The population of Sudan is about 28,000,000.

Tokyo and Yokohama conurbation: population about 28,000,000

Seoul: population more than 19,000,000

City outgrows Australia

Seoul, the capital of South Korea, is one of the largest and fastest growing cities in the world, with a population greater than that of the whole of Australia.

There are fewer people in the whole of Australia than there are in Seoul.

Each day, the world's population increases by nearly 240,000 – equivalent to one full Strahov Stadium.

A new crowd every day

Worldwide, on average, 382,650 babies are born and 144,902 people die every day. This means that, on average, the population of the world increases by 237,748 each day. That is almost enough people to fill the largest stadium in the modern world, the Strahov Stadium, in Prague, Czech Republic.

The world on an island

Allowing about 1 sq m (10.8 sq ft) per person, all the people in the world could stand shoulder to shoulder on the Indonesian island of Bali. The biggest problem would be getting them all there...

Bali has an area of about 5,620,000,000 sq m (60,495,156,000 sq ft) – slightly less than 1 sq m (10.8 sq ft) for each of the 5,734,000,000 people on Earth.

Bali

The Indonesian island of Bali would fit more than 1,394 times into Australia.

Stop shoving, will you? There's plenty of room!

Accelerated growth

The population of the world in 1500 was about 460,000,000, after centuries of slow growth. It then grew steadily until the middle of the 19th century, when it passed 1,000,000,000. It then began the incredible rise that has already enlarged it to more than 12 times the 1500 figure. In another 100 years it could almost double, to close to 11,000,000,000.

World population: expected to reach 11,000,000,000 in 2093, then level out

World population: expected to reach 10,000,000,000 in 2054, then grow much more slowly in the second half of the 21st century

World population: expected to reach 9,000,000,000 in 2035

World population: expected to reach 8,000,000,000 in 2021

World population: expected to reach 7,000,000,000 in 2009

World population: exceeded 6,000,000,000 in 1999

World population in 1995: 5,734,000,000

World population in 1985: 4,854,000,000

World population in 1980: 4,450,000,000

World population in 1970: 3,698,000,000

World population in 1960: 3,019,000,000

World population in 1950: 2,515,000,000

World population in 1900: 1,633,000,000

World population in 1850: 1,094,000,000

World population in 1800: 954,000,000

World population in 1700: 679,000,000

World population in 1600: 579,000,000

World population in 1500: 460,000,000

WORLD POPULATION (IN BILLIONS)

YEAR

1500   1600   1700   1800   1900   2000   2100

GROWTH AND AGE

"GREAT OAKS FROM little acorns grow." It is one of the marvels of nature that nearly all living things increase in size, often by a phenomenal factor of many millions from the seed or egg from which they originated. This growth can be extremely rapid and quite short-lived, or it can be very slow and extended over many years – over many centuries, even. Bamboo can grow as much in one day as one species of evergreen shrub might grow in 1,000 or more years. No animal lives anywhere near as long as the longest-lived trees or plants. Given the right conditions, however, some creatures can live for a surprisingly long time – including us humans, for whom a life span of 100 years is nowadays by no means unusual.

Bamboo shoots up twice as fast

Pacific giant kelp, a kind of seaweed, can grow as much as 45 cm (18 in) in one day. If you think that is a lot, try bamboo. Bamboo can grow at twice that rate – by the height of the average two-year-old child in one day. Bamboo grows so fast because it is actually a kind of grass found in tropical and semi-tropical countries with very high rainfalls – just think how the grass always seems to need cutting after a heavy downpour. Bamboo might grow twice as fast as Pacific giant kelp, but the kelp can eventually grow to twice the size of bamboo – and 34 times the height of the average man.

Pacific giant kelp can grow 45 cm (18 in) in one day.

Bamboo can grow 90 cm (3 ft) in one day.

The average two-year-old child is 84 cm (2 ft 9 in) tall.

Shrub grows ever so slowly

A 120-year-old specimen of *Dioon edule*, an evergreen shrub found in Mexico, was just 10 cm (4 in) tall, and growing at an almost imperceptible 0.76 mm (0.03 in) a year. At that rate it would take 1,184 years to grow as much as bamboo can grow in one day.

Pacific giant kelp can grow to 60 m (197 ft) – 34 times the height of the average man.

Bamboo can grow to 30 m (98 ft).

100 years

50 years

I think I'm going to need a bigger lawn mower!

The average man is 1.75 m (5 ft 9 in) tall.

One specimen of *Dioon edule* was found to be growing at only 0.76 mm (0.03 in) a year.

High and mighty

The tallest tree in the world is a coast redwood in Humboldt Redwoods State Park, California. Standing 110.6 m (363 ft) high, it is 17.6 m (58 ft) taller than the Statue of Liberty, and nearly twice as big as fully grown Pacific giant kelp. However, much taller eucalyptus trees were recorded in Australia in the 19th century – trees that were more than 130 m (426 ft) high.

Coast redwood: 110.6 m (363 ft) from base of trunk to top of tree

Statue of Liberty: 93 m (305 ft) from base of pedestal to torch

Pacific giant kelp: up to 60 m (197 ft)

Ancient trees outlive humans and animals

Most animals live much longer in captivity than they do in the wild, because in captivity they are well fed, receive regular medical attention, and are safe from predators. Over the years, human life expectancy has increased steadily, mainly because of advances in medicine. Today it is highest in rich, industrialized countries with good diets, and lowest in poor countries. We still have a long way to go to catch up the longest lived trees, however, which can live for 50 times as long as the oldest humans.

Mouse: up to six years

Trout: up to 10 years

Rabbit: up to 13 years

Dog: up to 20 years

Tiger: up to 26 years

Cow: up to 30 years

Polar bear: up to 38 years

Bison: up to 40 years

Rhinoceros: up to 50 years

Chimpanzee: up to 53 years

Hippopotamus: up to 54 years

Dolphin: up to 65 years

Eagle owl: up to 68 years

Indian elephant: up to 77 years

The average life expectancy for men in the USA is 72 years.

Women generally live longer than men. The average life expectancy for women in the USA is 75 years, and there are increasing numbers living for more than 100 years.

Growing together

From 50 cm (20 in) and 3.4 kg (7.5 lb) when born, the average human increases in height by slightly more than three times, and increases in weight by about 18 times. Although there are slight fluctuations, the growth rates of boys and girls remain similar until early adulthood, when men overtake women.

Female – six months: 66 cm (2 ft 2 in) 7.2 kg (16 lb)

Female – one year: 74 cm (2 ft 5 in) 9.1 kg (20 lb)

Female – two years: 84 cm (2 ft 9 in) 11.3 kg (25 lb)

Female – six years: 112 cm (3 ft 8 in) 20.4 kg (45 lb)

Female – 10 years: 137 cm (4 ft 6 in) 31.3 kg (69 lb)

Female – 14 years: 157 cm (5 ft 2 in) 48.5 kg (107 lb)

Female – 18 years: 165 cm (5 ft 5 in) 57 kg (126 lb)

Male – six months: 66 cm (2 ft 2 in) 7.7 kg (17 lb)

Male – one year: 74 cm (2 ft 5 in) 9.5 kg (21 lb)

Male – two years: 84 cm (2 ft 9 in) 11.8 kg (26 lb)

Male – six years: 114 cm (3 ft 9 in) 20.9 kg (46 lb)

Male – 10 years: 137 cm (4 ft 6 in) 31.3 kg (69 lb)

Male – 14 years: 157 cm (5 ft 2 in) 48.5 kg (107 lb)

Male – 18 years: 175 cm (5 ft 9 in) 64 kg (141 lb)

Slow clam

Clams are among the longest lived and slowest growing of all creatures. *Tindaria callistiformis*, a deep-sea clam, might take up to 100 years to reach only about 8 mm (0.3 in) in diameter.

Even after growing for 100 years, *Tindaria callistiformis* might fit on your fingernail.

Largest lifeform

The biggest living thing on Earth is a tree: the General Sherman giant sequoia, in Sequoia National Park, California. Its base is thicker than a giraffe is tall.

The General Sherman giant sequoia is about 8 m (26 ft) thick at its base.

Giraffe: 5.8 m (19 ft)

Growing up fast

Feeding on its mother's rich milk, a blue whale calf can gain 63 kg (139 lb) a day in its first year, and grow to nearly nine times its birth weight. A baby increasing its 3.4 kg (7.5 lb) birth weight by nearly nine times would weigh almost as much as a 10-year-old child after one year.

At birth a blue whale calf weighs up to 3 tonnes (3 tons).

After only one year a blue whale can weigh 26 tonnes (25.5 tons).

10-year-old girl: 31.3 kg (69 lb)

1-year-old girl: 9.1 kg (20 lb)

Kangaroos sure can grow

A newborn kangaroo, or joey, is about the size of a jelly baby. By the time it is fully grown it is some 30,000 times heavier than when it was born. The average newborn human baby weighs 3.4 kg (7.5 lb). An adult human 30,000 times heavier than this would weigh 102 tonnes (100 tons) – almost as much as a blue whale.

Joey drawn to scale of mother

Adult kangaroo: 20-30 kg (44-66 lb)

Joey (actual size): 0.75-1 g (0.026-0.035 oz)

Blue whale: 130 tonnes (128 tons)

Adult kangaroo drawn to scale of whale

Adult human drawn to scale of whale

102-tonne (100-ton) adult human

Crocodile man?

A 26-cm (10-in) baby Nile crocodile can grow 19 times as long, to become a 5-m (16-ft 5-in) adult. If humans grew like this, a 50-cm (20-in) baby would grow into a 9.5-m (31-ft) adult – more than five times as tall as the average man.

If humans grew like Nile crocodiles, a 50-cm (20-in) baby would grow up to become a 9.5-m (31-ft) giant.

5-m (16-ft 5-in) Nile crocodile

1.75-m (5-ft 9-in) man

Crocodile outgrows eagle

Golden eagles and Nile crocodiles both hatch from 8-cm (3-in) long eggs. However, a newly hatched Nile crocodile is twice as long as a newly hatched golden eagle, while a fully grown Nile crocodile can be nearly six times as long as a fully grown golden eagle.

Adult golden eagle: 88 cm (35 in) from beak to tail

Egg: 8 cm (3 in)

Chick: 13 cm (5 in)

Newly hatched Nile crocodile: 26 cm (10 in)

Adult Nile crocodile: up to 5 m (16 ft 5 in)

Egg: 8 cm (5 in)

The General Sherman giant sequoia is nearly 84 m (276 ft) tall – almost 50 times taller than the average man. Even a giraffe would need a ladder to reach its lowest branches.

Average man: 1.75 m (5 ft 9 in)

Giraffe: 5.8 m (19 ft)

Giant sequoia: up to 4,000 years

Bristlecone pine: more than 5,000 years

Olive tree: 3,000 years or more

Mountain Methuselah

Bristlecone pines can live for more than 5,000 years. The oldest living one is on Wheeler Peak, in Nevada, USA. Named Methuselah, after the old man in the Bible, it is thought to be 4,900 years old.

Giant tortoise: up to 100 years – maybe even 150

THE HUMAN BODY

THE AMAZING MACHINE that is the human body is full of surprises. Spread out flat, the average adult's skin is large enough to cover 10 copies of this book, front and back, while the air sacs in the lungs of three adults could cover a whole tennis court. Bone can withstand tremendous forces, but it is surprisingly light – when walking, the average adult presses down on each thighbone with the weight of an elephant, yet the whole skeleton accounts for only a sixth of the body's total weight. But perhaps the most remarkable organ in the human body is the brain, which triples in weight between birth and adulthood, until it weighs as much as the heart and both lungs put together. In relation to body size, the human brain is larger than the brain of any animal on Earth.

Big bones, little bones

You are born with about 300 bones in your body. As you grow, some of them fuse, until you have about 200 as an adult. The biggest bones, the thighbones, or femurs, are more than 150 times as long as the smallest, the stirrup bone, or stapes, inside each ear.

The average adult's thighbones are about 50 cm (20 in) long. This one is drawn actual size.

Grain of rice (actual size)

The average adult's stirrup bones are 3 mm (0.1 in) long – about as big as a grain of rice.

Bone can bear the weight

Bone is immensely strong – but then it needs to be. When walking, with each step an adult of average weight exerts a downward pressure on each thighbone of about 844 kg per sq cm (12,000 lb per sq in). Given that the thinnest part of the thighbone is about 2.5 cm (1 in) thick, this is equivalent to the weight of a bull African elephant. When running and jumping, the pressure on the thighbones is even greater.

A bull African elephant weighs about 5 tonnes (5 tons).

When walking, the average adult exerts a pressure on each thighbone equivalent to the weight of a bull African elephant.

Light as bone

Although bone is extremely strong, it is surprisingly light, accounting for only about a sixth of the average adult's overall body weight. Put another way, one person weighs the same as six skeletons – even more if that person is overweight.

The average man weighs 64 kg (141 lb) – as much as six skeletons.

The skeleton of the average man weighs only about 11 kg (24 lb).

Thighbone

Your body – the inside story

Most of us have only a vague idea of the locations of the main organs inside our bodies. For example, most people think the heart is on the left side of the chest, when in fact it is located centrally, between the lungs.

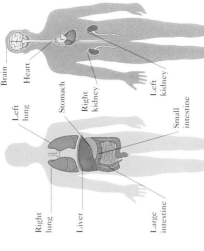

Brain
Heart
Left lung
Stomach
Right kidney
Left kidney
Right lung
Liver
Small intestine
Large intestine

Long in the tooth

If you have ever been unlucky enough to have had any teeth pulled out, you will know that they are much bigger than they look. This is because they have long roots that fix firmly into bony sockets under your gums. But even the largest human teeth are tiny compared with an elephant's massive chomping equipment.

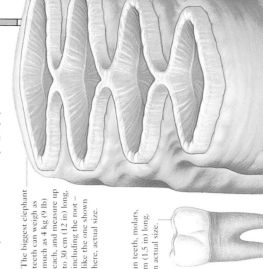

The biggest elephant teeth can weigh as much as 4 kg (9 lb) each, and measure up to 30 cm (12 in) long, including the root – like the one shown here, actual size.

The largest human teeth, molars, grow to up to 4 cm (1.5 in) long. This one is drawn actual size.

50 cm (20 in)

35 cm (14 in)

30 cm (12 in)

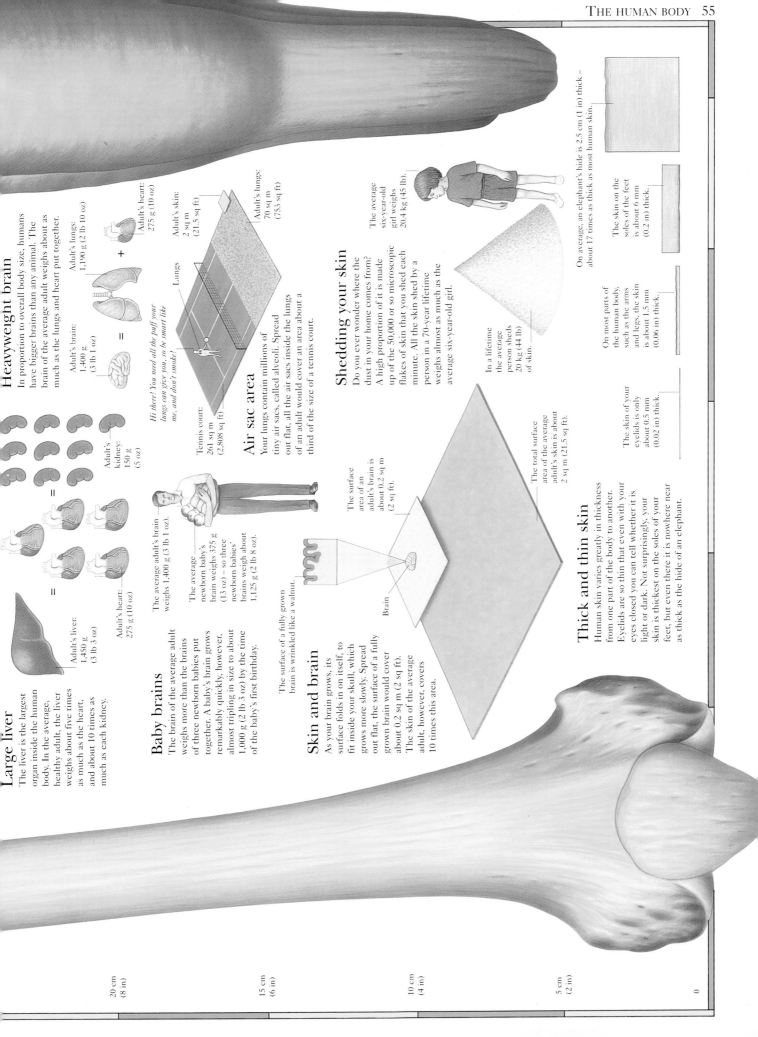

Large liver

The liver is the largest organ inside the human body. In the average, healthy adult, the liver weighs about five times as much as the heart, and about 10 times as much as each kidney.

Adult's liver: 1,450 g (3 lb 3 oz)

Adult's heart: 275 g (10 oz)

Adult's kidney: 150 g (5 oz)

Heavyweight brain

In proportion to overall body size, humans have bigger brains than any animal. The brain of the average adult weighs about as much as the lungs and heart put together.

Adult's brain: 1,400 g (3 lb 1 oz)

Adult's lungs: 1,190 g (2 lb 10 oz)

Adult's heart: 275 g (10 oz)

Baby brains

The brain of the average adult weighs more than the brains of three newborn babies put together. A baby's brain grows remarkably quickly, however, almost tripling in size to about 1,000 g (2 lb 3 oz) by the time of the baby's first birthday.

The average adult's brain weighs 1,400 g (3 lb 1 oz).

The average newborn baby's brain weighs 375 g (13 oz) – so three newborn babies' brains weigh about 1,125 g (2 lb 8 oz).

Air sac area

Your lungs contain millions of tiny air sacs, called alveoli. Spread out flat, all the air sacs inside the lungs of an adult would cover an area about a third of the size of a tennis court.

Hi there! You need all the puff your lungs can give you, so be smart like me, and don't smoke!

Lungs

Tennis court: 261 sq m (2,808 sq ft)

Adult's lungs: 70 sq m (753 sq ft)

Skin and brain

As your brain grows, its surface folds in on itself, to fit inside your skull, which grows more slowly. Spread out flat, the surface of a fully grown brain would cover about 0.2 sq m (2 sq ft). The skin of the average adult, however, covers 10 times this area.

The surface of a fully grown brain is wrinkled like a walnut.

Brain

The surface area of an adult's brain is about 0.2 sq m (2 sq ft).

The total surface area of the average adult's skin is about 2 sq m (21.5 sq ft).

Shedding your skin

Do you ever wonder where the dust in your home comes from? A high proportion of it is made up of the 50,000 or so microscopic flakes of skin that you shed each minute. All the skin shed by a person in a 70-year lifetime weighs almost as much as the average six-year-old girl.

In a lifetime the average person sheds 20 kg (44 lb) of skin.

The average six-year-old girl weighs 20.4 kg (45 lb).

Thick and thin skin

Human skin varies greatly in thickness from one part of the body to another. Eyelids are so thin that even with your eyes closed you can tell whether it is light or dark. Not surprisingly, your skin is thickest on the soles of your feet, but even there it is nowhere near as thick as the hide of an elephant.

The skin of your eyelids is only about 0.5 mm (0.02 in) thick.

On most parts of the human body, such as the arms and legs, the skin is about 1.5 mm (0.06 in) thick.

The skin on the soles of the feet is about 6 mm (0.2 in) thick.

On average, an elephant's hide is 2.5 cm (1 in) thick – about 17 times as thick as most human skin.

20 cm (8 in)

15 cm (6 in)

10 cm (4 in)

5 cm (2 in)

0

THE BODY AT WORK

ADVANCES IN MEDICAL SCIENCE mean that many of us can now expect to enjoy long, relatively healthy lives of 70 years or more. But nothing in medical science can match the natural miracle that sees us grow from a dot-size fertilized egg into a fully developed baby in the space of just 40 weeks. We are born with all our organs in full working order, and for most of us they will last, largely unaided, until our dying day. By then, they will have performed some incredible feats. Our lungs will have inhaled and exhaled enough air to fill either of the two largest airships ever built almost one-and-a-half times over. Our hearts will have beaten more than 2,500,000,000 times – pumping enough blood around the body to fill the fuel tanks of 700 jumbo jets in the process – and our stomachs and intestines will have digested the weight of six bull African elephants or more in food.

Every breath you take

When you do something strenuous, such as swimming or running, you breathe deeply and rapidly. At rest, you take shallower, less frequent breaths. When breathing normally, however, you take in about 500 cubic cm (30.5 cubic in) of air with each breath, at an average rate of 15 breaths a minute. Based on normal breathing, in a 70-year lifetime you will breathe about 275,000 cubic m (9,711,481 cubic ft) of air – enough to fill either of the two largest airships ever built almost one-and-a-half times over.

Every beat of your heart

Your heart is an amazingly strong and hard-wearing muscle. On average, it beats 70 times a minute, and pumps 59 cubic cm (3.6 cubic in) of blood with each beat. In a 70-year lifetime, that works out at more than 2,500,000,000 beats, pumping about 152,000,000 litres (33,435,987 gallons) of blood – enough to fill the fuel tanks of 10 Boeing 747 jumbo jets every year.

Elephantine appetites

The amount of food that people eat varies from person to person and from country to country, but in a 70-year lifetime the average person in a rich country such as the USA eats an estimated 30 tonnes (29.5 tons) of food – the weight of six bull African elephants.

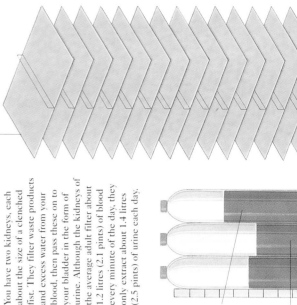

A bull African elephant weighs about 5 tonnes (5 tons) – so six of them weigh about 30 tonnes (29.5 tons).

The average man weighs 64 kg (141 lb). If he eats 30 tonnes (29.5 tons) of food in a 70-year lifetime, that works out at 469 times his adult body weight.

Like her sister ship *Hindenburg*, the 1930s airship *Graf Zeppelin II* was 245 m (804 ft) long, and held about 200,000 cubic m (7,062,895 cubic ft) of hydrogen. In a 70-year lifetime, the average person breathes enough air to fill *Graf Zeppelin II* almost one-and-a-half times over.

Hi! I think I'll stick to blowing up party balloons in future!

Your heart beats faster when you exercise, and slower when you rest, but on average it beats 70 times a minute.

The kidneys of the average adult weigh about 150 g (5 oz) each, and are about the size of a clenched fist.

When full, the fuel tanks of a jumbo jet hold 217,000 litres (47,734 gallons).

Vast area of vessels

As well as larger veins and arteries, your body contains millions of tiny blood vessels called capillaries. Minute tubes, each slightly more than 1 mm (0.04 in) long, they carry blood to all parts of your body. All the capillaries in the average adult's body form a huge network that, if spread out flat, would cover about 5,000 sq m (53,821 sq ft) – an area greater than that covered by 19 tennis courts.

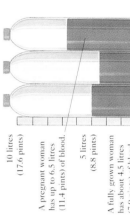

All the capillaries in the average adult's body could cover an area greater than 19 tennis courts.

Fist-size filters

You have two kidneys, each about the size of a clenched fist. They filter waste products and excess water from your blood, then pass these on to your bladder in the form of urine. Although the kidneys of the average adult filter about 1.2 litres (2.1 pints) of blood every minute of the day, they only extract about 1.4 litres (2.5 pints) of urine each day.

Every minute, the kidneys of the average adult filter about 1.2 litres (2.1 pints) of blood.

Each day, the kidneys of the average adult extract about 1.4 litres (2.5 pints) of urine from the blood.

2 litres (3.5 pints)

1 litre (1.8 pints)

0

The blood in your body

Blood might be thicker than water, but even a few drops of it can spread over a surprisingly large area – as you will know if you have ever cut yourself badly. Being generally smaller, women usually have less blood than men. When pregnant, however, a woman produces extra blood to supply her growing baby.

10 litres (17.6 pints)

A pregnant woman has up to 6.5 litres (11.4 pints) of blood.

5 litres (8.8 pints)

A fully grown woman has about 4.5 litres (7.9 pints) of blood.

A fully grown man has about 5 litres (8.8 pints) of blood.

0

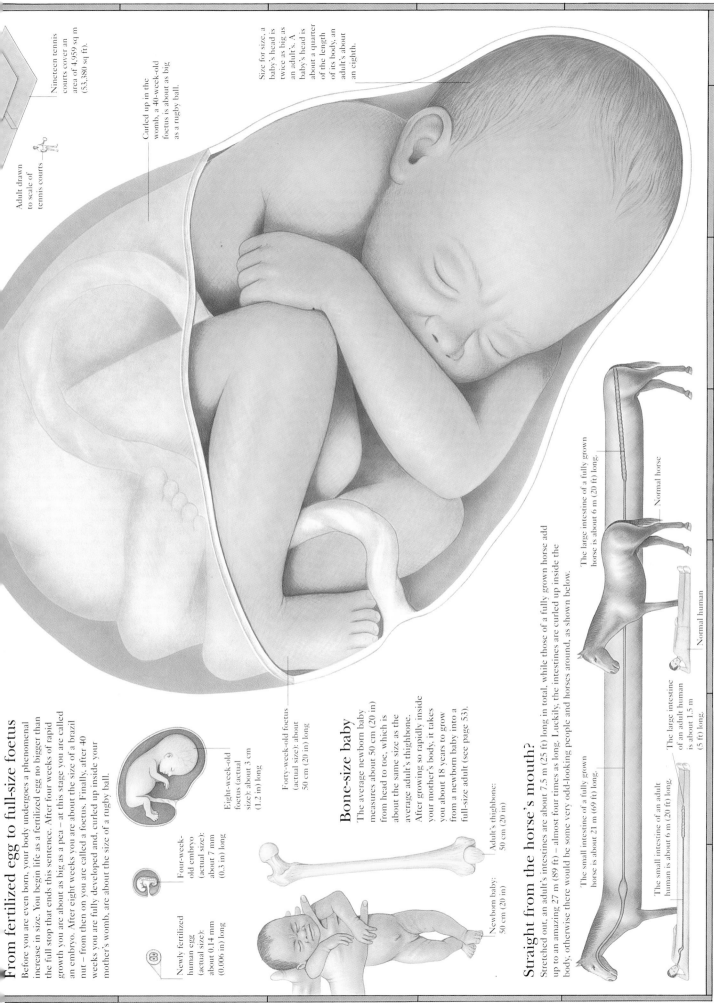

From fertilized egg to full-size foetus

Before you are even born, your body undergoes a phenomenal increase in size. You begin life as a fertilized egg no bigger than the full stop that ends this sentence. After four weeks of rapid growth you are about as big as a pea – at this stage you are called an embryo. After eight weeks you are about the size of a brazil nut – from then on you are called a foetus. Finally, after 40 weeks you are fully developed and, curled up inside your mother's womb, are about the size of a rugby ball.

Newly fertilized human egg (actual size): about 0.14 mm (0.006 in) long

Four-week-old embryo (actual size): about 7 mm (0.3 in) long

Eight-week-old foetus (actual size): about 3 cm (1.2 in) long

Forty-week-old foetus (actual size): about 50 cm (20 in) long

Nineteen tennis courts cover an area of 4,959 sq m (53,380 sq ft).

Adult drawn to scale of tennis courts

Curled up in the womb, a 40-week-old foetus is about as big as a rugby ball.

Size for size, a baby's head is twice as big as an adult's. A baby's head is about a quarter of the length of its body, an adult's about an eighth.

Bone-size baby

The average newborn baby measures about 50 cm (20 in) from head to toe, which is about the same size as the average adult's thighbone. After growing so rapidly inside your mother's body, it takes you about 18 years to grow from a newborn baby into a full-size adult (see page 53).

Newborn baby: 50 cm (20 in)

Adult's thighbone: 50 cm (20 in)

Straight from the horse's mouth?

Stretched out, an adult's intestines are about 7.5 m (25 ft) long in total, while those of a fully grown horse add up to an amazing 27 m (89 ft) – almost four times as long. Luckily, the intestines are curled up inside the body, otherwise there would be some very odd-looking people and horses around, as shown below.

The large intestine of a fully grown horse is about 6 m (20 ft) long.

Normal horse

The small intestine of a fully grown horse is about 21 m (69 ft) long.

Normal human

The small intestine of an adult human is about 6 m (20 ft) long.

The large intestine of an adult human is about 1.5 m (5 ft) long.

HUMANS AND ANIMALS

ARE HUMANS SUPERIOR to animals? When it comes to brain power, we like to think that we are well ahead of even the most intelligent animals, such as dolphins. Two ways in which we are clearly superior are our use of tools, and our ability to talk. Plainly, however, plenty of creatures are much stronger than we are – no human could ever beat a gorilla in a wrestling match. Nor are we necessarily physically superior to creatures that are much smaller than we are. Size for size, ants are even stronger than gorillas. Nor can we survive in such extreme environments as many animals can. Birds fly at altitudes where we would be unable to breathe, while sperm whales can swim at depths where the water pressure would quickly kill us. Only with the aid of machines can we safely venture into the worlds of these animals.

The 1.5-mm (0.06-in) common flea can jump almost 20 cm (8 in) high – equivalent to a 1.75-m (5-ft 9-in) man jumping 227.5 m (746 ft).

Airborne bacteria have been found alive and well at a height of 41,000 m (134,514 ft).

Enjoying the high life

Although many mountaineers have climbed the highest mountain in the world, Mt Everest, without special breathing equipment, humans are only able to ascend to greater heights in aircraft and balloons with the aid of oxygen. Some birds, however, appear to be able to fly at almost one-and-a-half times the height of Everest without difficulty. But the really high fliers are airborne bacteria, which have been found at almost five times the height of Everest.

Deep beneath the waves

Most humans cannot hold their breath underwater for more than a few seconds. Scuba divers cannot safely dive much below about 50 m (164 ft), because of the dangerous effects on the body of high water pressure. But some sea animals have no such problems. Sperm whales hunting giant squid might dive six times as deep as the Empire State Building is tall – holding their breath underwater for hours at a time.

Migrating whooper swans sometimes fly at more than 8,230 m (27,000 ft). But the record for high flying goes to the Rüppell's griffon, a kind of vulture. In 1973, above the Ivory Coast, a Rüppell's griffon collided with an aircraft at 11,278 m (37,000 ft).

Mt Everest, in the Himalayas, is 8,848 m (29,028 ft) high. It was first climbed in 1953, by Edmund Hillary and Sherpa Tenzing.

Toads live at up to 8,000 m (26,247 ft) in the Himalayas.

Jumping spiders have been found living at 6,706 m (22,000 ft) on Mt Everest.

Yaks are frequently seen at 6,000 m (19,685 ft) or more in the Himalayas.

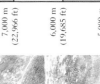

| 12,000 m (39,370 ft) |
| 11,000 m (36,089 ft) |
| 10,000 m (32,808 ft) |
| 9,000 m (29,528 ft) |
| 8,000 m (26,247 ft) |
| 7,000 m (22,966 ft) |
| 6,000 m (19,685 ft) |
| 5,000 m (16,404 ft) |

Tail feathers top hair

There are several recorded examples of women who have been able to grow their hair to more than twice their height. This achievement falls well short of the remarkable Japanese Phoenix fowl, however, which has been selectively bred over the years to grow longer and longer tail feathers – up to almost twice as long as a giraffe is tall.

Human hair grows about 1.2 cm (0.5 in) a month. Uncut, it usually stops growing when it is 60-90 cm (2-3 ft) long. But some women are able to grow their hair to nearly 4 m (13 ft).

The longest recorded tail feathers on a Japanese Phoenix fowl were an amazing 10.6 m (34 ft 9 in).

The mighty ant

A human can squash an ant under a fingertip but, size for size, ants are much stronger than we are. An ant can lift and carry about 50 times its own body weight. This is equivalent to a 64-kg (141-lb) man lifting 3,200 kg (7,055 lb) – about the weight of three family cars.

If humans were as strong as ants, a 64-kg (141-lb) man would be able to lift three family cars above his head.

Musclebound gorillas

Gorillas are up to eight times stronger than humans. If gorillas lifted weights, the world weightlifting record might be increased from 266 kg (586 lb) to 2,128 kg (4,691 lb).

In 1992, Li Yajuan, of China, set a new world weightlifting record for women of 150 kg (331 lb).

In 1988, Leonid Taranenko, of the then Soviet Union, set a new world weightlifting record for men of 266 kg (586 lb) – equivalent to lifting four 64-kg (141-lb) men above his head.

If gorillas lifted weights, they might be able to lift more than 2 tonnes (2 tons) – about the weight of two family cars.

The giraffe is the tallest animal in the world, growing up to 5.8 m (19 ft) in height.

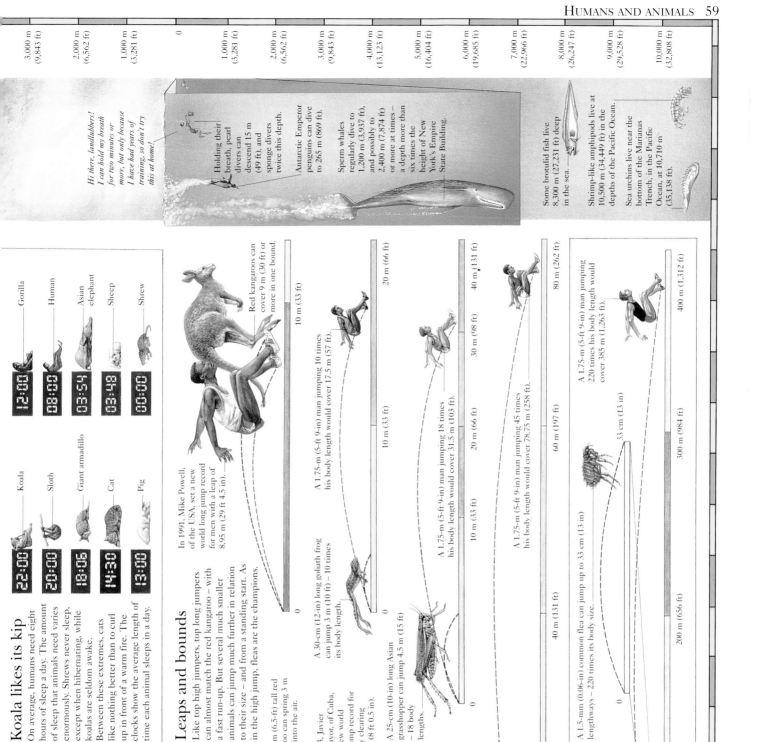

Depth/height scale (top):

3,000 m (9,843 ft)
2,000 m (6,562 ft)
1,000 m (3,281 ft)
0
1,000 m (3,281 ft)
2,000 m (6,562 ft)
3,000 m (9,843 ft)
4,000 m (13,123 ft)
5,000 m (16,404 ft)
6,000 m (19,685 ft)
7,000 m (22,966 ft)
8,000 m (26,247 ft)
9,000 m (29,528 ft)
10,000 m (32,808 ft)

Hi there, landlubbers! I can hold my breath for two minutes or more, but only because I have had years of training, so don't try this at home!

Holding their breath, pearl divers can descend 15 m (49 ft), and sponge divers twice this depth.

Antarctic Emperor penguins can dive to 265 m (869 ft).

Sperm whales regularly dive to 1,200 m (3,937 ft), and possibly to 2,400 m (7,874 ft) or more at times – a depth more than six times the height of New York's Empire State Building.

Some brotulid fish live 8,300 m (27,231 ft) deep in the sea.

Shrimp-like amphipods live at 10,500 m (34,449 ft) in the depths of the Pacific Ocean.

Sea urchins live near the bottom of the Marianas Trench, in the Pacific Ocean, at 10,710 m (35,138 ft).

Koala likes its kip

On average, humans need eight hours of sleep a day. The amount of sleep that animals need varies enormously. Shrews never sleep, except when hibernating, while koalas are seldom awake. Between these extremes, cats like nothing better than to curl up in front of a warm fire. The clocks show the average length of time each animal sleeps in a day.

12:00 — Koala
08:00 — Sloth
03:54 — Giant armadillo
03:48 — Cat
00:00 — Pig

22:00 — Gorilla
20:00 — Human
18:05 — Asian elephant
14:30 — Sheep
13:00 — Shrew

High achievers

Top high jumpers can leap almost as high as the Australian red kangaroo – yet are leaden-footed compared with some animals. While we struggle to jump above head-high – even with a run-up – the klipspringer antelope of southern Africa can jump 15 times its height. But fleas are the stars – from rest, a common flea can hop as high as 130 times its body size.

The 50-cm (20-in) tall klipspringer can jump 7.5 m (25 ft) high – equivalent to a 1.75-m (5-ft 9-in) man jumping 26.25 m (86 ft).

The 2-m (6.5-ft) tall red kangaroo can spring 3 m (10 ft) into the air.

In 1993, Javier Sotomayor, of Cuba, set a new world high jump record for men by clearing 2.45 m (8 ft 0.5 in).

Bulgarian Stefka Kostadinova set a new women's world high jump record of 2.09 m (6 ft 10.25 in) in 1987.

Leaps and bounds

Like top high jumpers, top long jumpers can almost match the red kangaroo – with a fast run-up. But several much smaller animals can jump much further in relation to their size – and from a standing start. As in the high jump, fleas are the champions.

In 1991, Mike Powell, of the USA, set a new world long jump record for men with a leap of 8.95 m (29 ft 4.5 in).

Red kangaroos can cover 9 m (30 ft) or more in one bound.

A 30-cm (12-in) long goliath frog can jump 3 m (10 ft) – 10 times its body length.

A 1.75-m (5-ft 9-in) man jumping 10 times his body length would cover 17.5 m (57 ft).

A 25-cm (10-in) long Asian grasshopper can jump 4.5 m (15 ft) – 18 body lengths.

A 1.75-m (5-ft 9-in) man jumping 18 times his body length would cover 31.5 m (103 ft).

A 10-cm (4-in) long jerboa, or desert rat, can jump 4.5 m (15 ft) – 45 times its body length.

A 1.75-m (5-ft 9-in) man jumping 45 times his body length would cover 78.75 m (258 ft).

Fleas jump the furthest

The amazing jumping abilities of *Pulex irritans*, the common flea, were measured in a series of experiments conducted by M. B. Mitzmain, a US scientist, in 1910.

A 1.5-mm (0.06-in) common flea can jump up to 33 cm (13 in) lengthways – 220 times its body size.

A 1.75-m (5-ft 9-in) man jumping 220 times his body length would cover 385 m (1,263 ft).

Scale markings (High achievers):
10 m (33 ft)
20 m (66 ft)
30 m (98 ft)
40 m (131 ft)
80 m (262 ft)
400 m (1,312 ft)

Scale markings (Leaps and bounds):
0
10 m (33 ft)
20 m (66 ft)
60 m (197 ft)
300 m (984 ft)

Scale markings (bottom):
0
10 m (33 ft)
0
20 m (66 ft)
0
40 m (131 ft)
0
33 cm (13 in)
0
100 m (328 ft)
200 m (656 ft)

PART TWO
THE WORLD IN ONE DAY

A DAY AROUND THE WORLD

WHAT HAPPENS IN ONE DAY in the life of the world? In the next 24 hours, the world will spin once on its axis and travel more than 2.5 million km (1.5 million miles) in its orbit round the Sun. As they hurtle through space, 2.5 billion people will spend the day at work, and 1 billion children will go to school. But what else is going on? This section gives you the figures for many of the other things that happen in an average day, from how much water an elephant drinks and how many times a flea can jump, to how many potatoes are harvested and how much gold is made into false teeth. So fasten your seat belt as we lift off into the bizarre world of real facts. Enjoy it, and remember . . . tomorrow is another day.

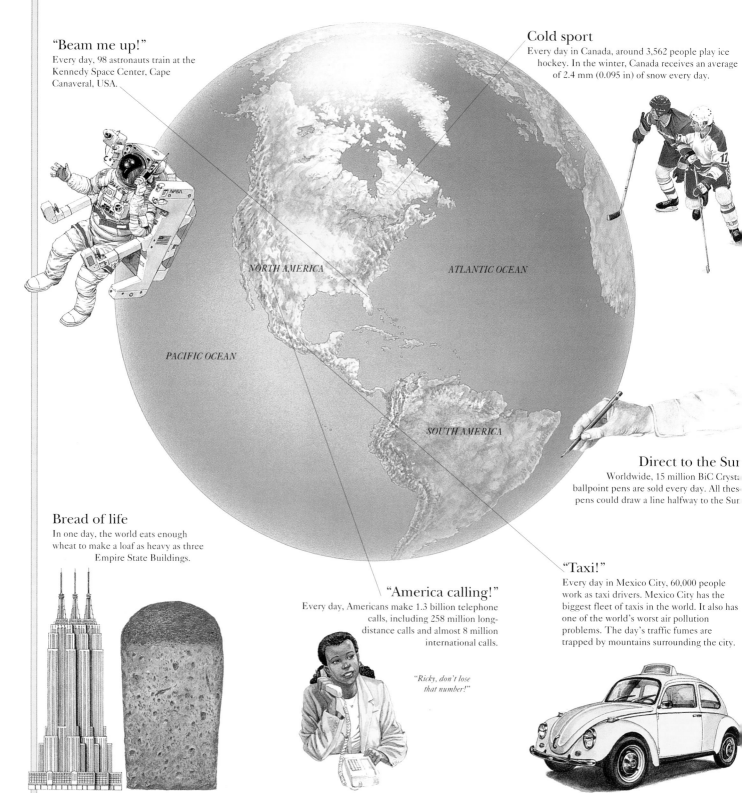

"Beam me up!"
Every day, 98 astronauts train at the Kennedy Space Center, Cape Canaveral, USA.

Cold sport
Every day in Canada, around 3,562 people play ice hockey. In the winter, Canada receives an average of 2.4 mm (0.095 in) of snow every day.

NORTH AMERICA

ATLANTIC OCEAN

PACIFIC OCEAN

SOUTH AMERICA

Direct to the Sun
Worldwide, 15 million BiC Crystal ballpoint pens are sold every day. All these pens could draw a line halfway to the Sun.

Bread of life
In one day, the world eats enough wheat to make a loaf as heavy as three Empire State Buildings.

"America calling!"
Every day, Americans make 1.3 billion telephone calls, including 258 million long-distance calls and almost 8 million international calls.

"Ricky, don't lose that number!"

"Taxi!"
Every day in Mexico City, 60,000 people work as taxi drivers. Mexico City has the biggest fleet of taxis in the world. It also has one of the world's worst air pollution problems. The day's traffic fumes are trapped by mountains surrounding the city.

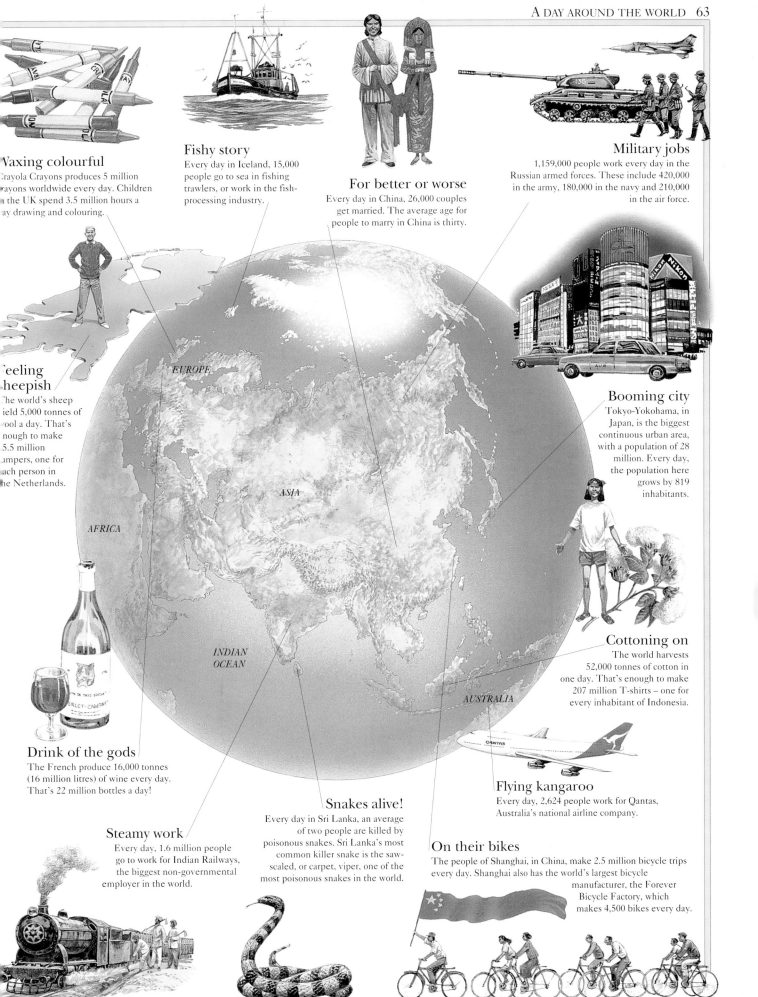

Waxing colourful
Crayola Crayons produces 5 million crayons worldwide every day. Children in the UK spend 3.5 million hours a day drawing and colouring.

Fishy story
Every day in Iceland, 15,000 people go to sea in fishing trawlers, or work in the fish-processing industry.

For better or worse
Every day in China, 26,000 couples get married. The average age for people to marry in China is thirty.

Military jobs
1,159,000 people work every day in the Russian armed forces. These include 420,000 in the army, 180,000 in the navy and 210,000 in the air force.

Feeling sheepish
The world's sheep yield 5,000 tonnes of wool a day. That's enough to make 5.5 million jumpers, one for each person in the Netherlands.

Booming city
Tokyo-Yokohama, in Japan, is the biggest continuous urban area, with a population of 28 million. Every day, the population here grows by 819 inhabitants.

Cottoning on
The world harvests 52,000 tonnes of cotton in one day. That's enough to make 207 million T-shirts – one for every inhabitant of Indonesia.

Drink of the gods
The French produce 16,000 tonnes (16 million litres) of wine every day. That's 22 million bottles a day!

Flying kangaroo
Every day, 2,624 people work for Qantas, Australia's national airline company.

Steamy work
Every day, 1.6 million people go to work for Indian Railways, the biggest non-governmental employer in the world.

Snakes alive!
Every day in Sri Lanka, an average of two people are killed by poisonous snakes. Sri Lanka's most common killer snake is the saw-scaled, or carpet, viper, one of the most poisonous snakes in the world.

On their bikes
The people of Shanghai, in China, make 2.5 million bicycle trips every day. Shanghai also has the world's largest bicycle manufacturer, the Forever Bicycle Factory, which makes 4,500 bikes every day.

PLANET EARTH

SINCE IT CAME INTO BEING around 4,600 million years ago, Planet Earth has continued to evolve every day. Heat from the Earth's core forces molten material to bubble to the surface in volcanoes. The plates that form the hard outer layers of the Earth grind against one another. The enormous pressure they exert pushes mountain ranges gradually higher, pulls the continents apart, and causes tremors and earthquakes. Wind, ice, and water wear away at rock, creating a landscape that is slowly changing day by day.

Volcanic energy

The energy released in one day by the eruption of Mount Tambora was reckoned to be 16,000 megatons – 800,000 times as powerful as the Hiroshima atom bomb.

Great balls of fire

Mount Vesuvius erupted in AD 79. Lava exploded into the air as ash and buried Pompeii. Its inhabitants were suffocated by poisonous gases. Ash then mixed with rain to create hot mud flows (lahars), which buried Herculaneum in just one day. The lethal lahars would have kept up with a modern Italian trying to escape on a moped.

"I'm burning rubber! Hey! Get this lahar off my tail!"

Earth in orbit

Planet Earth spins so fast on its axis that a person standing on the Equator is actually travelling at 1,670 kmh (1,038 mph) – the speed of Concorde – without moving at all.

Jupiter	Saturn	Neptune	Uranus	Earth	Mars	Pluto	Mercury	Venus
9h 55m	10h 39m	16h 7m	17h 14m	24h	24h 37m	6 days 9h	58 days 14h	244 days

How long is a day?

A day on Earth lasts 24 hours, but a day on Venus lasts eight Earth months, because Venus spins so slowly. Jupiter spins so fast that a day flashes by in under ten hours. An Earth watch would have to lose two minutes an hour to keep time on the Moon.

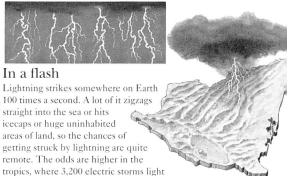

In a flash

Lightning strikes somewhere on Earth 100 times a second. A lot of it zigzags straight into the sea or hits icecaps or huge uninhabited areas of land, so the chances of getting struck by lightning are quite remote. The odds are higher in the tropics, where 3,200 electric storms light up the sky every 12 night hours.

Powering Nicaragua by tropical storms

Lightning power

If the power of all the tropical storms that take place in 24 hours could be harnessed, it would be equal to a full year's electricity consumption in a small country like Nicaragua.

Nightly fireworks

Stromboli is a volcano that has been active every day for thousands of years. The Ancients called it the Lighthouse of the Mediterranean because it produces a spectacular display of sizzling bombs and red fountains of lava against the night sky.

Mount Stromboli could go on erupting for hundreds of years before it becomes dormant and finally extinct.

The Bering Glacier in the Arctic began to retreat in the 1980s, raising fears about global warming. In 1993 it started to advance again.

The ice advances

Most glaciers are slow movers. They grind forward by about 2 m (6 ft) a day. The Bering Glacier in the Arctic is an exception. It advances an astonishing 91 m (300 ft) every day. It could transform a large back garden into a skating rink overnight.

Cosmic dust

Every day 110 tonnes of cosmic dust – debris from outer space – enters the Earth's atmosphere. If it could all be shovelled into one heap, it would be as big as a two-storey house.

America by storm

In one day, a hurricane could produce enough energy to replace the whole of the United States' electricity supply for nine months.

A day's work for the Sun

Every day the Sun beams four trillion kilowatt hours of energy to Earth. This recycles Earth's water by evaporation, causes winds, waves, and ocean currents, and is used in photosynthesis.

Powering the USA by hurricane

Squeaky clean

Enough rain falls to Earth every day for each one of its inhabitants to have a bath every five minutes.

Wet, wet, wet

If all the moisture in Earth's atmosphere fell as rain, it would produce 1,250 cu km (300 cu miles) of water. If all this rain fell in one day on the island of Manhattan, it would submerge it to a depth of 22 km (13.7 miles).

SMALL WORLD

Biosphere 2 is a huge greenhouse built in Arizona. Inside the Biosphere are areas of farmland, rainforest, desert, and even an ocean. This is the home of an experiment in global warming. Levels of carbon dioxide (CO_2) in Earth's atmosphere are rising. Scientists will steadily pump more CO_2 into Biosphere 2 in order to predict Earth's future.

Solar energy

It would take 167,000 nuclear power stations to produce the amount of energy that the Sun beams down to Earth in one day.

When the wind blows

Erosion is the wearing away and removal of land surfaces by running water, wind, or ice. Erosion is greatest in sloping areas and areas of little or no surface vegetation. On the west coast of Mauritania near Nouakchott, prevailing easterly winds carry 696,000 tonnes of sand and dust from the Sahara Desert into the Atlantic Ocean every day.

Cold snout

The end of a glacier is called the snout. At the snout, the ice either melts as fast as it arrives, or the glacier calves – bits break off to form icebergs. Jakobshavn Glacier in Greenland discharges 20 to 30 million tonnes of ice a day to the fiord at its snout.

Sand from the Sahara blows into the Atlantic from the west coast of Africa.

Icebergs calve at the snout of Jakobshavn Glacier in Greenland.

A raging torrent

The Iguaçu Falls are a string of 275 waterfalls on the border between Argentina and Brazil, close to Paraguay. The water of the Iguaçu River cascades down spectacular drops of up to 70 m (230 ft). At times of peak flow, enough water passes over the Falls to fill six Olympic swimming pools every second. However, in some years rainfall is so slight that this great river can dry up completely, as it did in 1978.

The Earth moves

An earthquake happens when rocks move along faults. Earthquakes are especially powerful when the tectonic plates that form the Earth's outer layers move against one another. The Great African Rift Valley in Djibouti experiences dozens of earthquakes every day, indicating the continuous movement of the tectonic plates beneath Africa.

A DAY TO REMEMBER

Up to your ears

The wettest day ever was 15 March 1952, when 190 cm (74 in) of torrential rain fell at Cilaos on the island of La Réunion in the Indian Ocean.

It drove them quackers

On 14 July 1953, golf ball-sized hailstones fell in a freak storm in Alberta, Canada. Powered by gale-force winds, they bashed to death 36,000 ducks.

Piste off

The biggest snowfall ever was recorded on 7 February 1963, when 198 cm (78 in) of snow fell at Mile 47 Camp, Cooper River Division, Alaska, USA.

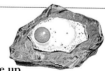

Sunny side up

On 13 September 1922 the temperature in the shade at al'Aziziyah in the Libyan desert reached 57.8°C (136°F) – hot enough to fry an egg on a rock.

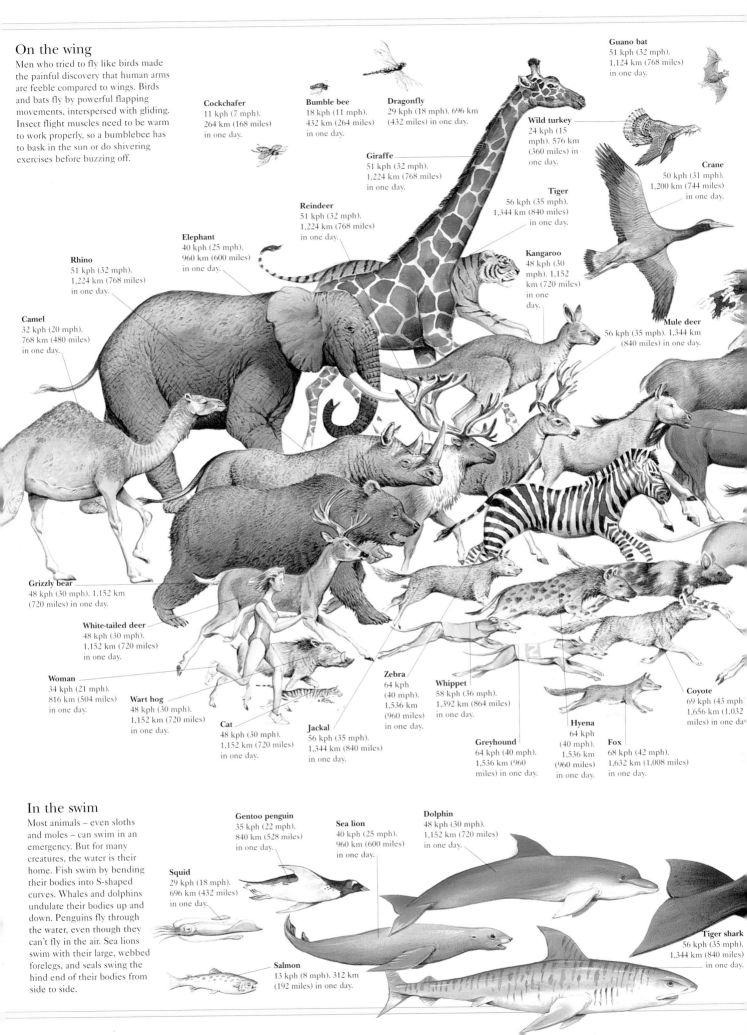

On the wing

Men who tried to fly like birds made the painful discovery that human arms are feeble compared to wings. Birds and bats fly by powerful flapping movements, interspersed with gliding. Insect flight muscles need to be warm to work properly, so a bumblebee has to bask in the sun or do shivering exercises before buzzing off.

Guano bat
51 kph (32 mph). 1,124 km (768 miles) in one day.

Cockchafer
11 kph (7 mph). 264 km (168 miles) in one day.

Bumble bee
18 kph (11 mph). 432 km (264 miles) in one day.

Dragonfly
29 kph (18 mph). 696 km (432 miles) in one day.

Wild turkey
24 kph (15 mph). 576 km (360 miles) in one day.

Crane
50 kph (31 mph). 1,200 km (744 miles) in one day.

Giraffe
51 kph (32 mph). 1,224 km (768 miles) in one day.

Tiger
56 kph (35 mph). 1,344 km (840 miles) in one day.

Reindeer
51 kph (32 mph). 1,224 km (768 miles) in one day.

Kangaroo
48 kph (30 mph). 1,152 km (720 miles) in one day.

Elephant
40 kph (25 mph). 960 km (600 miles) in one day.

Mule deer
56 kph (35 mph). 1,344 km (840 miles) in one day.

Rhino
51 kph (32 mph). 1,224 km (768 miles) in one day.

Camel
32 kph (20 mph). 768 km (480 miles) in one day.

Grizzly bear
48 kph (30 mph). 1,152 km (720 miles) in one day.

White-tailed deer
48 kph (30 mph). 1,152 km (720 miles) in one day.

Woman
34 kph (21 mph). 816 km (504 miles) in one day.

Wart hog
48 kph (30 mph). 1,152 km (720 miles) in one day.

Cat
48 kph (30 mph). 1,152 km (720 miles) in one day.

Jackal
56 kph (35 mph). 1,344 km (840 miles) in one day.

Zebra
64 kph (40 mph). 1,536 km (960 miles) in one day.

Whippet
58 kph (36 mph). 1,392 km (864 miles) in one day.

Greyhound
64 kph (40 mph). 1,536 km (960 miles) in one day.

Hyena
64 kph (40 mph). 1,536 km (960 miles) in one day.

Fox
68 kph (42 mph). 1,632 km (1,008 miles) in one day.

Coyote
69 kph (43 mph). 1,656 km (1,032 miles) in one day.

In the swim

Most animals – even sloths and moles – can swim in an emergency. But for many creatures, the water is their home. Fish swim by bending their bodies into S-shaped curves. Whales and dolphins undulate their bodies up and down. Penguins fly through the water, even though they can't fly in the air. Sea lions swim with their large, webbed forelegs, and seals swing the hind end of their bodies from side to side.

Gentoo penguin
35 kph (22 mph). 840 km (528 miles) in one day.

Sea lion
40 kph (25 mph). 960 km (600 miles) in one day.

Dolphin
48 kph (30 mph). 1,152 km (720 miles) in one day.

Squid
29 kph (18 mph). 696 km (432 miles) in one day.

Salmon
13 kph (8 mph). 312 km (192 miles) in one day.

Tiger shark
56 kph (35 mph). 1,344 km (840 miles) in one day.

ANIMALS

A LOUD CHORUS of birdsong shakes the animal kingdom from its slumber as the first rays of the Sun touch the treetops. The animals' day centres around key survival activities: defending territory, hunting or foraging for food, and feeding young. Mammals, birds, and winged insects also spend time grooming to keep their bodies clean and healthy. Monkeys and apes groom each other to cement friendships; a cow may indulge in 180 bouts of grooming in one day!

Hummingbird
Up to 5,400 wingbeats a minute.

Bat
Up to 1,200 wingbeats a minute.

Sparrow
600 wingbeats a minute.

Butterfly
Up to 640 wingbeats a minute.

Swift
360 wingbeats a minute.

Stork
180 wingbeats a minute.

In a flap
Most birds, insects, and bats need to beat their wings rapidly in order to stay in the air. A hummingbird's wings beat so quickly you can hardly see them.

Pygmy shrew
Up to 2 million heartbeats a day.

Mouse
720,000 heartbeats a day.

Elephant
43,200 heartbeats a day.

Frog
43,200 heartbeats a day.

Heartbeats
Astonishingly, all mammals other than humans have around 800 million heartbeats in a lifetime. An elephant's heart beats 20–30 times a minute, so it will have "used up" its heartbeats after about 50 years. At the other end of the scale, a pygmy shrew's heart beats 900–1,400 times a minute; its lifespan is about 1.5 years.

Rabbit
288,000 heartbeats a day.

Hedgehog
432,000 heartbeats a day.

Hedgehog hibernating
4,320 heartbeats a day.

On the run
Animals run to escape predators and to chase prey. This race of slowcoaches and speedy creatures shows how far animals could travel if they were able to sprint along at their top speeds for a whole 24 hours.

Three-toed sloth
110 m (360 ft) per hour. 3 km (2 miles) in one day.

Rosy boa
0.3 kph (0.2 mph). 7 km (4 miles) in one day.

Pig
18 kph (11 mph). 432 km (264 miles) in one day.

Squirrel
19 kph (12 mph). 463 km (288 miles) in one day.

Wild turkey
24 kph (15 mph). 1,200 km (744 miles) in one day.

Yellow-bellied sea snake
3 kph (2 mph). 77 km (48 miles) in one day.

Giant tortoise
370 m (1,214 ft) per hour. 9 km (6 miles) per day.

Common shrew
5 kph (3 mph). 116 km (72 miles) in one day.

Chicken
15 kph (9 mph). 348 km (216 miles) in one day.

Animal appetites
For some creatures, eating is hard work. The African elephant spends about 18 hours out of 24 feeding and drinking. The giant anteater chomps its way through 30,000 ants in one day, and the sperm whale swallows a whole tonne of squid. Others just sit back and let it happen. Moles feed on unsuspecting bypassers that drop into their tunnels.

Vampire bat
Drinks two tablespoons of blood every day, the equivalent of half its own bodyweight.

Mole
Eats its own weight (50–80 g/ 2–3 oz) of food every day.

Anteater
Eats more than 30,000 ants in one day.

Giant panda
Eats 10–45 kg (22–99 lb) of bamboo shoots in one day.

Bull elephant
Eats 227 kg (500 lb) of foliage in one day. Drinks 80–160 litres (18–35 gallons) of water.

BEES' WORLD
As the Sun rises, a beehive starts to buzz with activity. The youngest workers clean the hive. After three days, they are promoted to feeding the larvae. After ten days, their job is to build the comb, and after 16 days, they start filling the comb with pollen and nectar. After 20 days, they guard the entrance of the hive, and finally they leave the hive to gather nectar. The queen bee lays 1,500 eggs a day.

Blue whale
Absorbs five tonnes of krill (tiny crustaceans) in one day.

PLANTS

WITHOUT PLANTS, THERE WOULD BE no life on Earth. Plants produce oxygen, which all creatures need to breathe and to convert food into energy. Their fruits, leaves, and seeds give us food and medicines. Their fibres are woven into clothes. Their juices give us drinks and dyes. Trunks and branches provide shelter, fuel, and material for furniture and tools. So far, we have identified 500,000 plants, and still more await discovery. Yet large areas of natural vegetation are disappearing. Every day, 36,000 hectares (89,000 acres) of tropical rainforest are destroyed. But just one Amazonian Brazil nut tree can produce more nutritious food than can be cultivated on the land that is cleared when the tree is felled.

Plant growth

Plants harness energy from the Sun's rays, turning it into glucose, which they use to grow. This process is called photosynthesis. A large rainforest tree can produce 1.5 kg (3 lb) of pure glucose in one day, using just sunlight and water. Some plants, like those on the left, grow very quickly. Compared with these plants, even the fastest-growing trees seem to grow slowly. Some of the slowest-growing plants are lichens (see bottom right), which can take a century to grow just 2.5 cm (1 in)!

Morning glory

The flowers of morning glory last only one day. They open in the morning and shrivel and die towards evening. Plants flower by responding to the number of hours of daylight in a day. A light-sensitive pigment in the leaves sends a hormone signal to the flowerbuds, triggering them to open.

Giant bamboo

A native of Burma, the giant bamboo can grow an astonishing 46 cm (18 in) a day. Bamboo is technically a grass. Its stems are used for making buckets, rafts, and chopsticks. In India and Southeast Asia, the bamboo harvest is turned into 4,800 tonnes of paper a day.

Giant kelp

Giant kelp is a huge seaweed found in the coastal waters of California. It grows up to 45 cm (18 in) per day. Fronds of kelp form underwater forests, and can reach 100 m (328 ft), making it the tallest plant in the world.

Callie grass

Callie grass grows 15 cm (6 in) in one day.

Titan arum

The centre of the titan arum shoots up 7.5 cm (3 in) in a day. Its flowers last just one day, giving off a stench of rotting flesh. In its native Sumatra, the titan arum is known as the "corpse flower".

Eucalyptus deglupta

This eucalyptus is the world's fastest-growing tree. It can spurt 2.5 cm (1 in) in a day. One specimen in New Zealand reached 10.6 m (35 ft) in 15 months.

SMALL WORLD

The Royal Botanic Gardens at Kew, near London, UK, house 40,000 living plants, including a growing example of one in eight of all known flowers, and more than 6 million dried plants (nine out of ten of all species). This is the largest collection of plants in the world. Many of the plants grow in one of several greenhouses at Kew. The greenhouses recreate the conditions of different climates from around the world, ranging from hot desert to cold alpine. Many visitors to Kew feel as if they have travelled the globe in just one day.

Giant puffball

The giant puffball fungus can measure up to 2m (6.6 ft) in circumference, and weigh up to 20 kg (44 lb). If an animal or a raindrop strikes the fungus, spores (seeds) are puffed out of a hole in the top. In just one day, a giant puffball can release 7 billion spores.

Fairy ring

A toadstool springs from underground filaments called a mycelium. Some toadstools appear as if by magic, in a circle overnight, as the mycelia grows out from a central point. These formations are often called "fairy rings".

Diesel tree

The copaiba tree, which grows in the Amazon, contains an oil similar to diesel. It can produce 9 litres (2 gallons) of this oil every hour. So one tree could yield 218 litres (48 gallons) of fuel in one day, enough to fill the petrol tanks of five cars! Diesel trees are now being cultivated in Japan for their oil.

Petroleum nut

The petroleum nut tree, which grows in Borneo and the Philippines, produces a high-octane oil in its seeds. The seeds of one tree yield 53 litres (12 gallons) a year, which is about three teaspoonsful every day. The oil is burned in lamps, and was used by the Japanese during World War II to fuel tanks.

Petroleum plant

Petroleum seed

Rubber tree

When a cut is made in the bark of a rubber tree, a sticky white liquid called latex oozes out. Rubber trees flourish in the warm, moist climates of Malaysia, Indonesia, and Thailand. They produce more than 18,000 tonnes of rubber every day.

Oak

Oak trees live to a great age – one in Switzerland is thought to be around 930 years old. A mature oak tree draws 90 litres (20 gallons) of water out of the earth every day. Oak trees are very slow-growing, putting on only 1.4 mm (0.055 in) in one day.

Trumpet tree
Saplings of the trumpet tree growing on the rainforest floor shoot up towards the light at a rate of 7 mm (0.28 in) in one day.

Rampant growth

Tropical rainforest grows twice as fast as temperate oakwood. Every hectare of warm, wet rainforest produces 75 kg (165 lb) of lush new growth per day (67 lb per acre). Each hectare (2.5 acres) of rainforest contains 300 tonnes of 180 different species of tree, one tonne of plants, one tonne of earthworms, and 8 kg (18 lb) of birds.

Tasmanian cider gum
One of the fastest-growing of all trees, the cider gum (native to Tasmania) can grow 4 mm (0.16 in) taller every day.

Bristlecone pine
The bristlecone pine grows very slowly, at only 0.009 mm (0.00035 in) a day. This tree is very long-lived. One specimen is believed to be 4,600 years old.

Lichens
Lichens are extremely slow growers, putting on 0.0025 mm (0.0001 in) a day.

Poplar
A poplar tree grows just over 3 mm (0.118 in) taller every day.

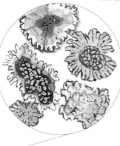

Sleepy creatures

Some animals sleep almost all day long, and others hardly sleep at all. The amount of sleep an animal needs depends partly on how it feeds. The sleepy koala bear has a low-energy diet of leaves, and snoozes for around 22 hours out of 24. The tiny shrew is a carnivore that has to feed almost constantly to survive, leaving precious little time for dozing.

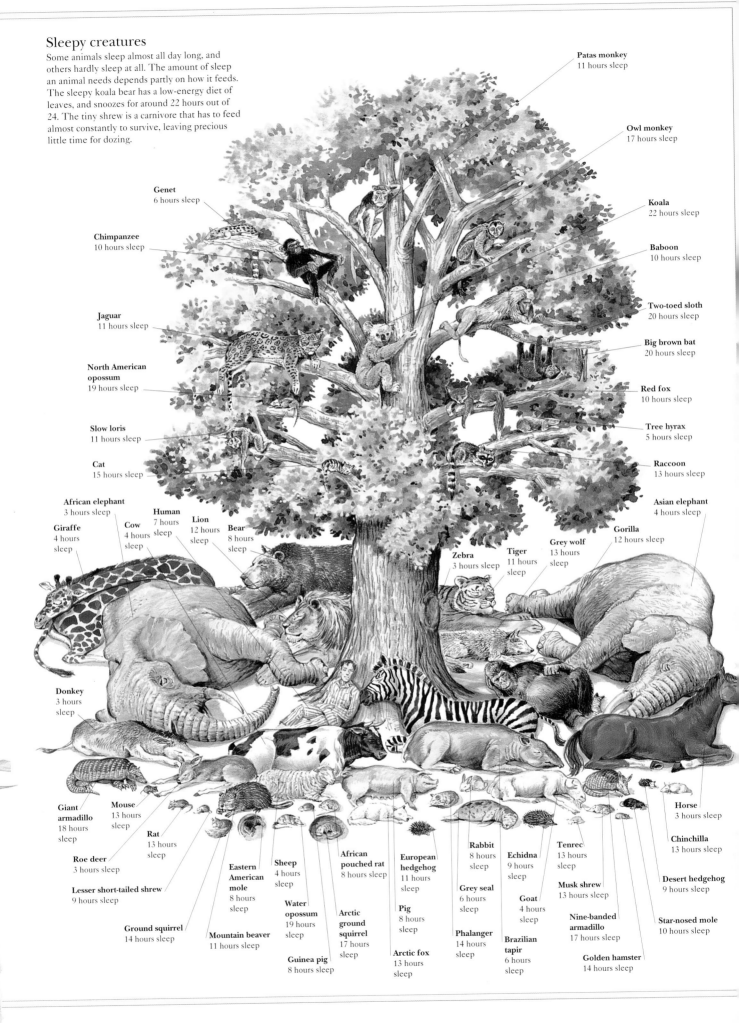

Patas monkey
11 hours sleep

Owl monkey
17 hours sleep

Koala
22 hours sleep

Baboon
10 hours sleep

Two-toed sloth
20 hours sleep

Big brown bat
20 hours sleep

Red fox
10 hours sleep

Tree hyrax
5 hours sleep

Raccoon
13 hours sleep

Asian elephant
4 hours sleep

Gorilla
12 hours sleep

Grey wolf
13 hours sleep

Tiger
11 hours sleep

Zebra
3 hours sleep

Genet
6 hours sleep

Chimpanzee
10 hours sleep

Jaguar
11 hours sleep

North American opossum
19 hours sleep

Slow loris
11 hours sleep

Cat
15 hours sleep

African elephant
3 hours sleep

Giraffe
4 hours sleep

Cow
4 hours sleep

Human
7 hours sleep

Lion
12 hours sleep

Bear
8 hours sleep

Donkey
3 hours sleep

Giant armadillo
18 hours sleep

Mouse
13 hours sleep

Rat
13 hours sleep

Roe deer
3 hours sleep

Lesser short-tailed shrew
9 hours sleep

Ground squirrel
14 hours sleep

Eastern American mole
8 hours sleep

Mountain beaver
11 hours sleep

Sheep
4 hours sleep

Water opossum
19 hours sleep

Guinea pig
8 hours sleep

African pouched rat
8 hours sleep

Arctic ground squirrel
17 hours sleep

European hedgehog
11 hours sleep

Pig
8 hours sleep

Arctic fox
13 hours sleep

Rabbit
8 hours sleep

Grey seal
6 hours sleep

Phalanger
14 hours sleep

Echidna
9 hours sleep

Goat
4 hours sleep

Brazilian tapir
6 hours sleep

Tenrec
13 hours sleep

Musk shrew
13 hours sleep

Nine-banded armadillo
17 hours sleep

Golden hamster
14 hours sleep

Horse
3 hours sleep

Chinchilla
13 hours sleep

Desert hedgehog
9 hours sleep

Star-nosed mole
10 hours sleep

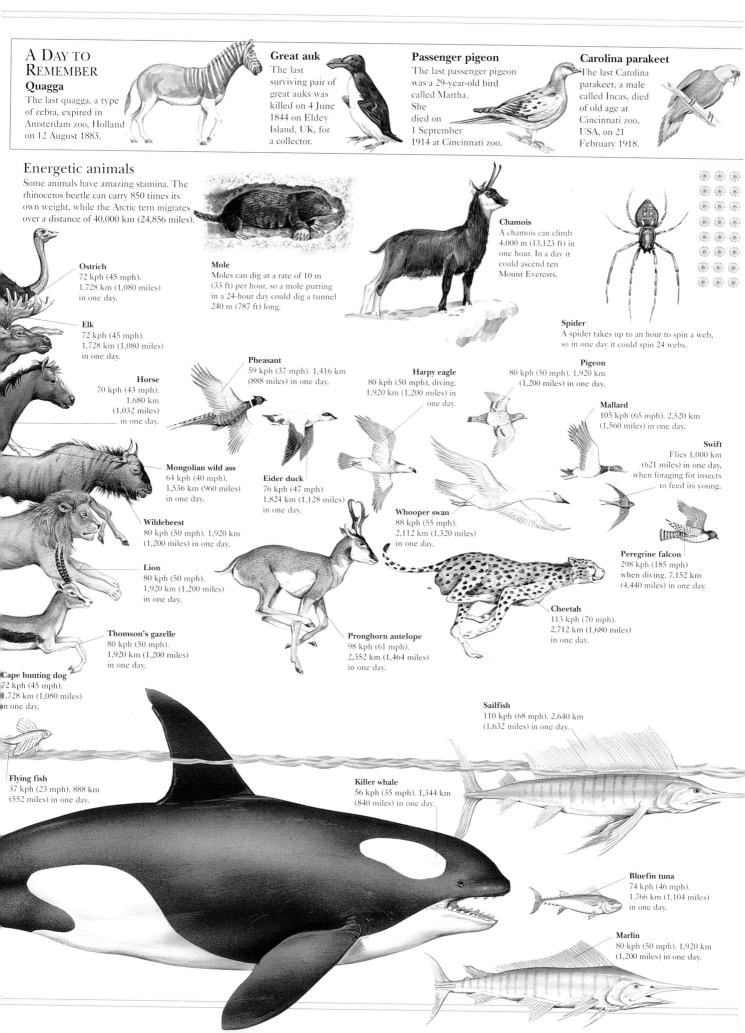

A DAY TO REMEMBER

Quagga
The last quagga, a type of zebra, expired in Amsterdam zoo, Holland on 12 August 1883.

Great auk
The last surviving pair of great auks was killed on 4 June 1844 on Eldey Island, UK, for a collector.

Passenger pigeon
The last passenger pigeon was a 29-year-old bird called Martha. She died on 1 September 1914 at Cincinnati zoo.

Carolina parakeet
The last Carolina parakeet, a male called Incas, died of old age at Cincinnati zoo, USA, on 21 February 1918.

Energetic animals

Some animals have amazing stamina. The rhinoceros beetle can carry 850 times its own weight, while the Arctic tern migrates over a distance of 40,000 km (24,856 miles).

Mole
Moles can dig at a rate of 10 m (33 ft) per hour, so a mole putting in a 24-hour day could dig a tunnel 240 m (787 ft) long.

Chamois
A chamois can climb 4,000 m (13,123 ft) in one hour. In a day it could ascend ten Mount Everests.

Spider
A spider takes up to an hour to spin a web, so in one day it could spin 24 webs.

Ostrich
72 kph (45 mph). 1,728 km (1,080 miles) in one day.

Elk
72 kph (45 mph). 1,728 km (1,080 miles) in one day.

Horse
70 kph (43 mph). 1,680 km (1,032 miles) in one day.

Pheasant
59 kph (37 mph). 1,416 km (888 miles) in one day.

Harpy eagle
80 kph (50 mph), diving. 1,920 km (1,200 miles) in one day.

Pigeon
80 kph (50 mph). 1,920 km (1,200 miles) in one day.

Mallard
105 kph (65 mph). 2,520 km (1,560 miles) in one day.

Swift
Flies 1,000 km (621 miles) in one day, when foraging for insects to feed its young.

Mongolian wild ass
64 kph (40 mph). 1,536 km (960 miles) in one day.

Eider duck
76 kph (47 mph) 1,824 km (1,128 miles) in one day.

Wildebeest
80 kph (50 mph). 1,920 km (1,200 miles) in one day.

Whooper swan
88 kph (55 mph). 2,112 km (1,320 miles) in one day.

Peregrine falcon
298 kph (185 mph) when diving. 7,152 km (4,440 miles) in one day.

Lion
80 kph (50 mph). 1,920 km (1,200 miles) in one day.

Thomson's gazelle
80 kph (50 mph). 1,920 km (1,200 miles) in one day.

Pronghorn antelope
98 kph (61 mph). 2,352 km (1,464 miles) in one day.

Cheetah
113 kph (70 mph). 2,712 km (1,680 miles) in one day.

Cape hunting dog
72 kph (45 mph). 1,728 km (1,080 miles) in one day.

Sailfish
110 kph (68 mph). 2,640 km (1,632 miles) in one day.

Flying fish
37 kph (23 mph). 888 km (552 miles) in one day.

Killer whale
56 kph (35 mph). 1,344 km (840 miles) in one day.

Bluefin tuna
74 kph (46 mph). 1,766 km (1,104 miles) in one day.

Marlin
80 kph (50 mph). 1,920 km (1,200 miles) in one day.

THE HUMAN BODY

EVERY DAY, THE HUMAN BODY needs refuelling with oxygen, food, and water. The body's powerhouse is the brain. It accounts for only 2 per cent of body weight, but uses 20 per cent of our oxygen intake, 20 per cent of our calorie intake, and 15 per cent of the body's blood supply. To fight disease, each body produces 10 billion new white blood cells a day. Skin cells last for 25 days, red blood cells survive for 120 days, liver cells for 500 days, and some nerve cells last a whole lifetime. The continual process of cell renewal that keeps the body alive is called metabolism.

Body factory

The digestive system, lungs, and kidneys are at work around the clock. The digestive system breaks down food into particles so tiny that blood can take nourishment to all parts of the body. The body's entire blood supply passes through the lungs almost once a minute, collecting and distributing oxygen. Waste products are removed from the blood in the kidneys, each of which contains around one million tiny filters called nephrons.

Breathtaking stuff

Each one of us takes around 30,000 breaths a day. If you expelled all the air you breathed in a day into rubber dinghies, you would be able to inflate 50 two-person dinghies in 24 hours.

Bloodbath

The average human heart beats 100,800 times a day. The amount of blood that passes through the heart each day would fill 170 baths.

House of skin

We shed approximately one million dead skin cells every 40 minutes. One person will shed enough skin in a lifetime to fill a suitcase. All the skin shed by the world's people in one day would fill a four-storey house.

Body heat

The total body heat produced in one day by a human being is enough to power a light bulb for a day and a half.

Supersperm

One man's testicles produce nearly 300 million sperm cells each day. This means that (in theory!) it would take only 23 men just one day to produce enough sperm to reproduce the entire world population.

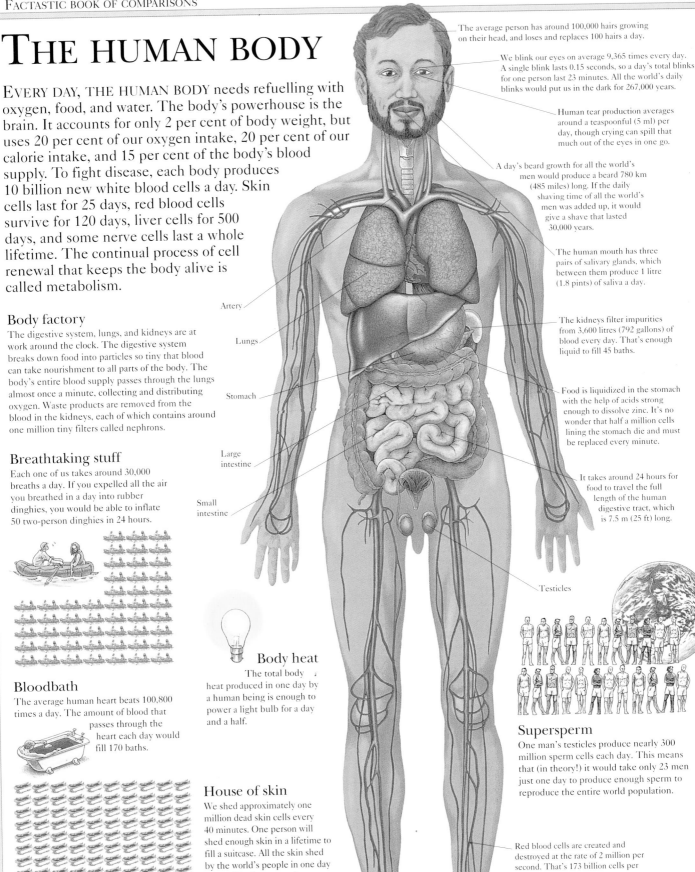

The average person has around 100,000 hairs growing on their head, and loses and replaces 100 hairs a day.

We blink our eyes on average 9,365 times every day. A single blink lasts 0.15 seconds, so a day's total blinks for one person last 23 minutes. All the world's daily blinks would put us in the dark for 267,000 years.

Human tear production averages around a teaspoonful (5 ml) per day, though crying can spill that much out of the eyes in one go.

A day's beard growth for all the world's men would produce a beard 780 km (485 miles) long. If the daily shaving time of all the world's men was added up, it would give a shave that lasted 30,000 years.

The human mouth has three pairs of salivary glands, which between them produce 1 litre (1.8 pints) of saliva a day.

The kidneys filter impurities from 3,600 litres (792 gallons) of blood every day. That's enough liquid to fill 45 baths.

Food is liquidized in the stomach with the help of acids strong enough to dissolve zinc. It's no wonder that half a million cells lining the stomach die and must be replaced every minute.

It takes around 24 hours for food to travel the full length of the human digestive tract, which is 7.5 m (25 ft) long.

Red blood cells are created and destroyed at the rate of 2 million per second. That's 173 billion cells per person per day.

Nails grow at up to 0.1 mm (0.004 in) per day from a bed of active cells under the skin folds at their base and sides. Fingernails grow up to four times faster than toenails, and both grow faster in warm weather than in cold.

Artery

Lungs

Stomach

Large intestine

Small intestine

Testicles

SMALL WORLD

The human body is host to many different kinds of microorganism, including eyebrow mites and amoebas that swim on our teeth. Around 10 billion bacteria live on the skin and 15 trillion bacteria live in our digestive system.

Fleas can jump 14,400 times a day in search of food, and lay up to 1,000 eggs a day.

A tick can spend a whole day feeding on human blood, and then – after it drops off the skin – a whole year without feeding again.

Tapeworms can live in the small intestine. Every day, hundreds of eggs drop off the worm and are passed in the faeces.

The head louse can live on the scalp. It lays up to ten eggs, called nits, every day. Head lice feed on blood that they suck through the skin.

Mother's milk

A commercial dairy cow yields 18 litres (31 pints) of milk a day. It would take 25 nursing mothers to produce as much milk in one day as a single commercial dairy cow.

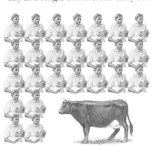

Grand flush

The body produces around 1.7 litres (3 pints) of urine a day. The total daily world production of human urine would take a full 20 minutes to pass over Niagara Falls. If everyone in the world spent five minutes a day in the only loo in the world, that loo would be engaged for 57,000 years!

It wasn't me!

The human digestive system expels 2 litres (3.5 pints) of gas every day. The average fart is composed of 59% nitrogen, 21% hydrogen, 9% carbon dioxide, 7% methane and 4% oxygen. That means the world releases enough hydrogen in its daily farts to fill 13 Hindenburg airships.

Around 1,000 brain cells are lost per head per day. But cell losses hardly slow down the nerve impulses of the brain, which travel at around 290 kph (180 mph).

Brainy

During waking hours, the brain constantly perceives and interprets information from the senses, then initiates a response. The brain uses more than 100 billion neurons (nerve cells) every day, and more than 100 trillion synapses (nerve connections) to perform these complex functions.

Sleep tight

While you are awake, you are aware of what you are doing – you are conscious. When you sleep, your conscious brain switches off, but other parts continue the vital task of keeping you alive. In a 24-hour period, the average person spends seven hours asleep. The entire world population spends just over 5 million years asleep every night!

Transatlantic nails

If all the world's finger- and toenails could be joined together to make one gigantic nail, in just one day it would grow almost from London to New York.

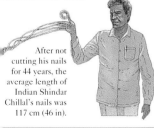

After not cutting his nails for 44 years, the average length of Indian Shindar Chillal's nails was 117 cm (46 in).

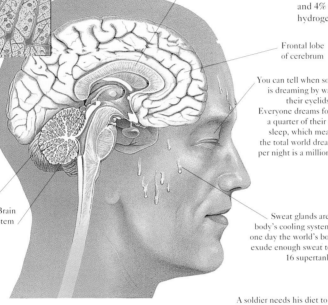

White matter, made up of nerve fibres

Frontal lobe of cerebrum

Cerebellum

Brain stem

You can tell when someone is dreaming by watching their eyelids move. Everyone dreams for about a quarter of their nightly sleep, which means that the total world dream time per night is a million years!

Sweat glands are the body's cooling system. In one day the world's bodies exude enough sweat to fill 16 supertankers.

What a stink!

All the human excrement produced in one day would weigh around one million tonnes. It would fill the enormous Louisiana Superdome, New Orleans, to a depth of 19 m (62 ft).

A male office worker needs to consume 2,400 Cal (10,080 kJ) every day.

A policeman on the beat needs to eat 2,800 Cal (11,760 kJ) every day.

A soldier needs his diet to supply at least 3,500 Cal (14,700 kJ) a day.

American theatre

American operating theatres are the busiest in the world. Around 197,000 operations take place in American hospitals every day. These include 1,679 hysterectomies, 381 hip replacements, 15,052 eye operations, 17,372 heart operations, 523 skin grafts, 285 brain operations, and 2,463 ear operations.

Eating for energy

The energy given by the food we eat is measured in calories (Cal) and kilojoules (kJ). Active people need more calories each day than people who sit to work, though the body burns energy even during sleep to keep the metabolism going.

A DAY TO REMEMBER

Discovery of X-ray

Photographic rays that pass through flesh but not through bone were discovered by William Röntgen on 8 November 1895, but not used medically until later.

First operation with anaesthetic

On 30 March 1842, Dr Crawford Long of Georgia, USA, removed a cyst from the neck of James M. Venable using ether as an anaesthetic.

First vaccination

The first vaccination was carried out by Dr Edward Jenner, a British doctor, on 14 May 1796. Eight-year-old James Phipps was vaccinated with cowpox as protection against smallpox.

WORLD POPULATION

THE WORLD'S POPULATION IS EXPLODING FAST, with more people being born and living longer than ever before. By 1999, there were mor than 6 billion people on Earth. The human boom is set to continue – especially in Africa, Asia, and Latin America – until, in 2080, it will peak at just over 10 billion. The world's population first began to rocke about 10,000 years ago, when people began to grow their own food. The birth rate soared again in the West during the 1800s with the scientific advances of the Industrial Revolution. New methods of growing and transporting food meant that more people ate a better diet. There were also fewer deaths in childhood. Today, 12 times more people are added to the population of the world every day than 100 years ago.

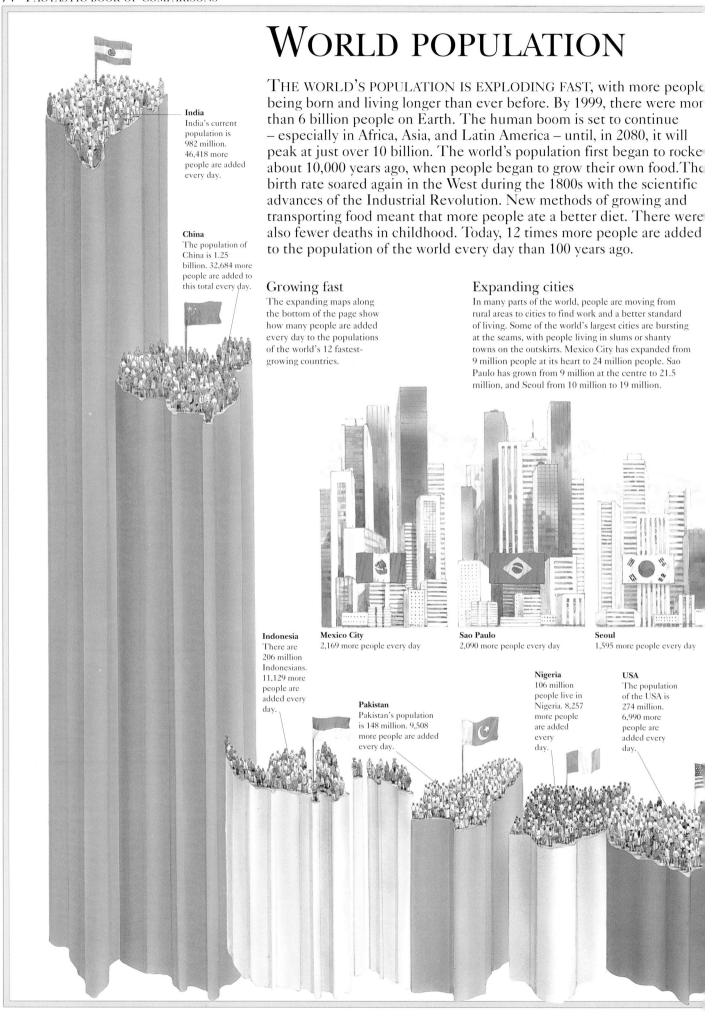

India
India's current population is 982 million. 46,418 more people are added every day.

China
The population of China is 1.25 billion. 32,684 more people are added to this total every day.

Growing fast

The expanding maps along the bottom of the page show how many people are added every day to the populations of the world's 12 fastest-growing countries.

Expanding cities

In many parts of the world, people are moving from rural areas to cities to find work and a better standard of living. Some of the world's largest cities are bursting at the seams, with people living in slums or shanty towns on the outskirts. Mexico City has expanded from 9 million people at its heart to 24 million people. Sao Paulo has grown from 9 million at the centre to 21.5 million, and Seoul from 10 million to 19 million.

Mexico City
2,169 more people every day

Sao Paulo
2,090 more people every day

Seoul
1,595 more people every day

Indonesia
There are 206 million Indonesians. 11,129 more people are added every day.

Pakistan
Pakistan's population is 148 million. 9,508 more people are added every day.

Nigeria
106 million people live in Nigeria. 8,257 more people are added every day.

USA
The population of the USA is 274 million. 6,990 more people are added every day.

A DAY TO REMEMBER

Baby in a tube

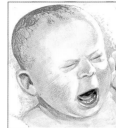

The first test-tube baby was Louise Brown. She was born in Oldham, in the UK, on 25 July 1978.

"We do!"

The largest ever wedding was conducted by Sun Myung Moon in Seoul, Korea, on 25 August 1995. He married 35,000 couples in the Olympic Stadium, and 325,000 other couples around the world by satellite link.

Dead cold

Dr James Bedford was the first person to be frozen after death, on 12 January 1967, in accordance with the science of cryonics. His body will be defrosted when a cure is found for the illness that killed him.

Dead end

Every day around the world, nearly 150,000 people breathe their last and die. Many die of old age, some perish in accidents or are murdered, while fatal diseases kill the rest.

Heart disease
33,000 die every day

Diarrhoea
14,000 die every day

Cancer
13,500 die every day

A whale of a day

The total weight of all the 364,321 babies born in the world in one day is 690 tonnes. This is the same weight as five blue whales.

Pneumonia
13,500 die every day

Tuberculosis
8,200 die every day

Malaria
5,800 die every day

Measles
4,000 die every day

Whooping cough
1,400 die every day

SMALL WORLD

China has more people than any other country on Earth, with a population of 1.2 billion. Overcrowding, and a shortage of resources including food, health care, and education, has caused the Chinese government to restrict family sizes in order to slow population growth rate. Chinese couples are encouraged to postpone marriage until their late 20s. In some areas, parents are allowed to have one child only.

Happy birthday!

Every day across the world, 16.5 million people celebrate their birthday. In many countries, people mark the day with a feast or party. To mark a first birthday in Korea, the child sits at a table with various objects on it – whichever he or she picks up is said to determine the child's future. Many Buddhists celebrate their birthdays by taking gifts of food to monks, and by releasing fish, turtles, and birds at the temple.

Births and deaths

In one day all over the world, 364,321 people are born and 147,137 people die. So every day there are 217,184 more people on Earth.

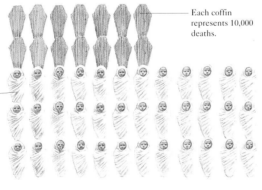

Each coffin represents 10,000 deaths.

Each baby in swaddling clothes represents 10,000 births.

Crowded planet

A hundred years from now, 378,000 people will be born every day, and 324,000 people will die. So every day, there will be 54,000 more people on Earth. In 1996, the world birth rate was 25 per 1,000, and the death rate, nine per 1,000. In 2100, the World Bank predicts that the birth rate will be down to 13 per 1,000 and the death rate up to 11 per 1,000.

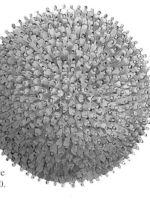

Brazil
166 million people live in Brazil. 6,757 more are added every day.

Bangladesh
Bangladesh has a population of 125 million. 6,186 more people are added every day.

Iran
66 million people live in Iran. 4,945 more people are added every day.

Mexico
Mexico has a population of 96 million. 4,789 more people are added every day.

Ethiopia
60 million people live in Ethiopia. 4,661 more people are added every day.

Vietnam
Vietnam's population is 78 million. 4,315 more people are added every day.

ONE DAY'S FOOD

IT WOULD TAKE 75 SUPERTANKERS to carry one day's food for the entire planet. Most people rely on wheat, rice, and maize for their basic food. Adults need around 2,500 calories of food energy a day. However, while Westerners consume up to 4,000 calories a day, some Africans struggle on barely 1,800 calories each. And every day, 35,000 people die of starvation. Nutritious vegetables may hold the answer to the world's food needs. A field of soya beans yields 30 times as much body-building protein as a field on which beef cattle are reared.

738,000 beef cattle are slaughtered every day.

The world slaughters 3 million pigs a day.

1.4 million sheep are slaughtered every day.

104 million chickens are slaughtered every day worldwide.

Meat

Every day, the world eats 604,000 tonnes of meat, the same weight as a herd of a million cows. But if everyone had a share of the world's meat, there would be barely enough for two mouthfuls a day each.

Potatoes
We dig up 675,000 tonnes of potatoes every day.

Food city

This is what the world's daily helpings of some of its most nutritious foodstuffs would look like, delivered into the heart of a modern city.

Grapes
The world's grape harvest for one day weighs 157,000 tonnes – that's over 22 billion individual grapes.

Beans and lentils
In one day, the world produces 156,000 tonnes of beans and lentils.

Bananas
The world's daily banana harvest is 160,000 tonnes.

Cabbages
The world produces 132,000 tonnes of cabbages in a day.

Watermelons
Every day 130,000 tonnes of watermelons are harvested.

Cocoa
The world produces 8,000 tonnes of cocoa beans every day. That's enough to make over 700 million bars of chocolate.

Peas
Every day, the world harvests 19,000 tonnes of peas. That's enough to serve 500 million people with a portion of peas.

The fastest food in the world

Every day, Americans get through seven million pizzas, 4,000 tonnes of potato crisps, 400 tonnes of pretzels, 300,000 tins of Spam, around 15 million burgers, 15 million litres (26 million pints) of ice cream, 250 million Coca-Colas, as well as five chips each.

Coca-Cola

Chips

Burgers

Ice cream

Pretzels

Pizza

Tea
Worldwide over 8,000 tonnes of tea leaves are produced every day. That's enough for three billion cups of tea.

Cucumbers
The world grows more than 73,000 tonnes of cucumbers every day. That's enough for everyone in India and China to have a cucumber sandwich each.

Onions
The world's daily onion harvest weighs over 110,000 tonnes, as much as the largest ocean liner afloat.

Salt
The world harvests 500,000 tonnes of salt in a day.

Eggs

Eggs are a complete food because they provide all the proteins the body needs for tissue growth and repair. Today, China is the world's biggest egg-producing nation. The world's hen population lays over two billion eggs a day. They would make an omelette as big as the island of Cyprus.

Japan
The Japanese eat 25,000 tonnes of fish a day.

France
The French love the pungent flavour of garlic. France produces 126 tonnes of garlic every day.

China
The Chinese lead the world in rice production. They eat rice at every meal, getting through 530,000 tonnes every day.

Greece
The Greeks eat more bread than anyone else in the world – 300 g (9 oz) per person per day.

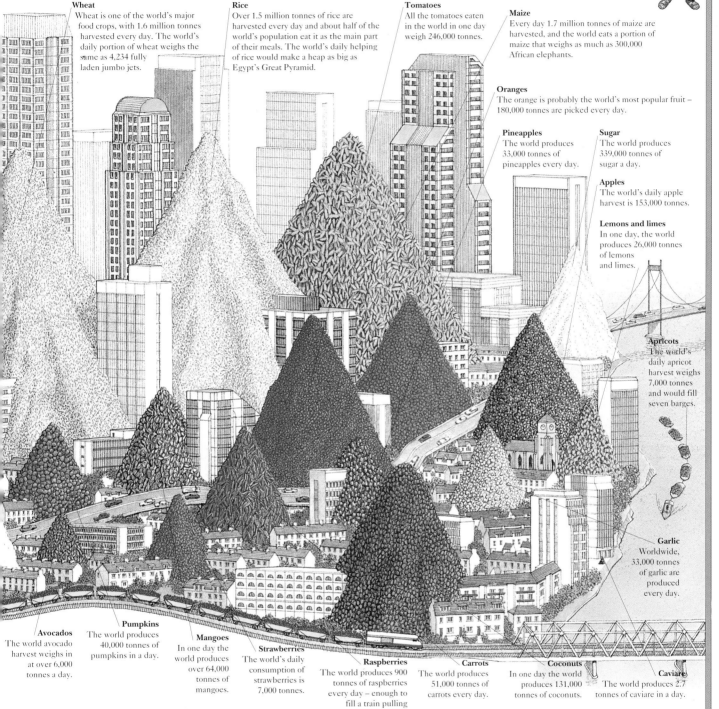

Wheat
Wheat is one of the world's major food crops, with 1.6 million tonnes harvested every day. The world's daily portion of wheat weighs the same as 4,234 fully laden jumbo jets.

Rice
Over 1.5 million tonnes of rice are harvested every day and about half of the world's population eat it as the main part of their meals. The world's daily helping of rice would make a heap as big as Egypt's Great Pyramid.

Tomatoes
All the tomatoes eaten in the world in one day weigh 246,000 tonnes.

Maize
Every day 1.7 million tonnes of maize are harvested, and the world eats a portion of maize that weighs as much as 300,000 African elephants.

Oranges
The orange is probably the world's most popular fruit – 180,000 tonnes are picked every day.

Pineapples
The world produces 33,000 tonnes of pineapples every day.

Sugar
The world produces 339,000 tonnes of sugar a day.

Apples
The world's daily apple harvest is 153,000 tonnes.

Lemons and limes
In one day, the world produces 26,000 tonnes of lemons and limes.

Apricots
The world's daily apricot harvest weighs 7,000 tonnes and would fill seven barges.

Garlic
Worldwide, 33,000 tonnes of garlic are produced every day.

Avocados
The world avocado harvest weighs in at over 6,000 tonnes a day.

Pumpkins
The world produces 40,000 tonnes of pumpkins in a day.

Mangoes
In one day the world produces over 64,000 tonnes of mangoes.

Strawberries
The world's daily consumption of strawberries is 7,000 tonnes.

Raspberries
The world produces 900 tonnes of raspberries every day – enough to fill a train pulling 23 cars.

Carrots
The world produces 51,000 tonnes of carrots every day.

Coconuts
In one day the world produces 131,000 tonnes of coconuts.

Caviare
The world produces 2.7 tonnes of caviare in a day.

High-flying food
Nearly three million meals are served in the air every day.

Honey
In one day, bees sip the nectar from three trillion flowers. They make more than 3,000 tonnes of honey, enough to spread a slice of toast as big as London.

OUT OF THIS WORLD
The first astronauts ate cold paste which they squeezed from a tube. Today's astronauts have a menu of more than 70 items. Some of these are in cans or foil bags. Others need water to be added. Many are heated before eating. Astronauts eat from trays strapped to their laps.

PRODUCTION

THE WORLD IS A mighty production machine; every day its factories and offices churn out more than £50 billion worth of stuff. It's strange to think that machines were invented less than 300 years ago, and before that time, everything was made at home, by hand. The first machines were powered by renewable energy – the sweat of human effort, and water turning a wheel. But the age of steam was fired by coal, so the first really efficient machines began to gobble up the Earth's natural resources. Today, the world uses the equivalent of 4 kg (8 lb) of oil per person a day – though Americans consume five and a half times that amount!

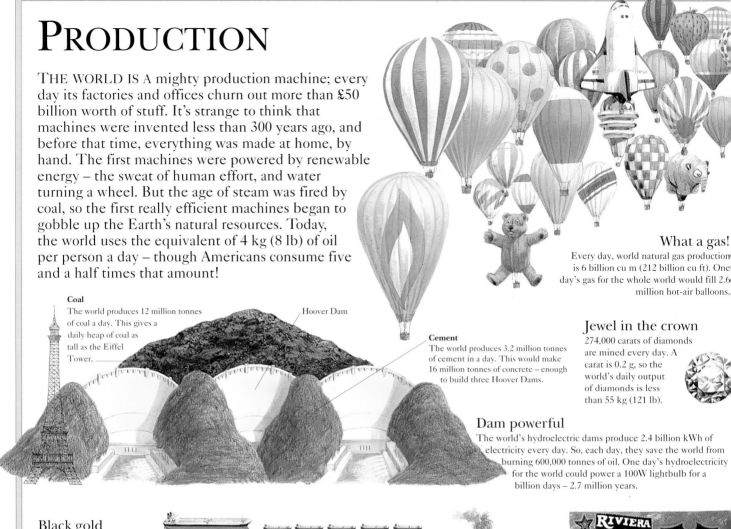

What a gas!
Every day, world natural gas production is 6 billion cu m (212 billion cu ft). One day's gas for the whole world would fill 2.6 million hot-air balloons.

Coal
The world produces 12 million tonnes of coal a day. This gives a daily heap of coal as tall as the Eiffel Tower.

Hoover Dam

Cement
The world produces 3.2 million tonnes of cement in a day. This would make 16 million tonnes of concrete – enough to build three Hoover Dams.

Jewel in the crown
274,000 carats of diamonds are mined every day. A carat is 0.2 g, so the world's daily output of diamonds is less than 55 kg (121 lb).

Dam powerful
The world's hydroelectric dams produce 2.4 billion kWh of electricity every day. So, each day, they save the world from burning 600,000 tonnes of oil. One day's hydroelectricity for the world could power a 100W lightbulb for a billion days – 2.7 million years.

Black gold
The world produces almost nine million tonnes of oil a day, which is enough to fill the holds of 90 supertankers. Every day in the world's refineries, 2.3 million tonnes of oil is turned into petrol, and 1.4 million tonnes is used to manufacture plastics.

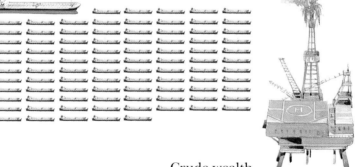

Cars, cars cars
Every day, a staggering 141,132 vehicles roll off the world's production lines. The USA is the world's biggest car manufacturer, but the people of Luxembourg own more cars per head than any other nation in the world. In Luxembourg, there are 57 cars on the road for every 100 people.

Crude wealth
A typical oil rig can pump up 189,000 barrels of precious crude oil from the Earth every day.

Neon city
A nuclear power station could produce enough electricity in a day to supply the city of Las Vegas for eight years.

USA
The USA produces 32,326 vehicles a day.

Japan
Japan manufactures 28,345 vehicles every day.

France
The French manufacture 9,837 vehicles daily.

Germany
13,268 vehicles roll off Germany's production lines each day.

South Korea
In South Korea, 7,706 vehicles are produced every day.

Canada
Every day Canada's factories produce over 6,567 vehicles.

Spain
Spain manufactures 6,609 vehicles a day.

UK
5,272 vehicles roll out of the assembly plant every day in the UK.

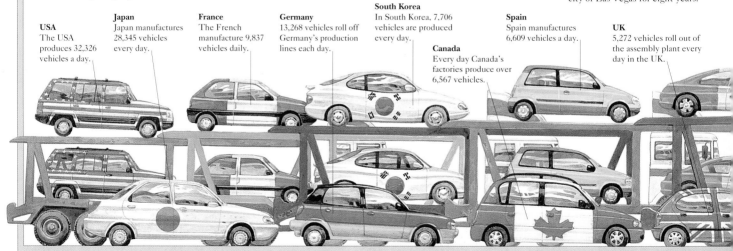

Awesome ores

Metals are extracted from ores, naturally occurring minerals that are mined from the Earth.

The world produces 50,000 tonnes of copper every day. That would make enough copper piping to encircle the globe three times.

73,000 tonnes of aluminium are produced in a day, enough to make almost 5 billion coke cans.

The world's mines yield 90 tonnes of uranium every day. Uranium is used to power nuclear reactors.

Daily world production of platinum is 80 kg (176 lb). It is used in electrical instruments and jewellery.

The world output of mercury is 11 tonnes a day, enough to fill nearly seven million thermometers.

Gold rush

6.75 tonnes of gold is mined in one day – more than a quarter of it comes from South Africa. Gold is so dense that the world's daily gold extraction could fit inside a fridge. Every day, 150 kg (330 lb) of gold (much of it recycled) is used to fill teeth – that's the weight of more than 2 adults.

A new car every day

The number of cars in the world is increasing at a little more than half the rate of world population growth. Every day, at least one new car is produced for every other additional person on the planet.

Italy
4,234 vehicles are manufactured in Italy every day.

Brazil
Brazil produces 4,966 vehicles daily.

Great heaps of stuff

If all the tonnes of different stuff produced in the world in a single day could be piled up into heaps, the landscape would be dominated by mountains of useful goods. The daily soap powder heap would be big enough to ski down, and one day's timber pile would reach right up into outer space.

Steel
Around two million tonnes of steel are produced every day. If all this steel was turned into cars, it would make 2.5 million vehicles in one day.

Computers
IBM manufactures 20,000 computers a day.

Soap powder
54,000 tonnes of soap and washing powder are produced in a day. That would be enough to wash two loads of laundry for each US citizen.

Washing machines
The world churns out 101,000 washing machines a day.

Tyres
2.3 million tyres are manufactured every day, almost a quarter of them in the USA.

Fridges
Worldwide, 137,000 fridges are made every day.

String
If you made the world's daily harvest of around 10,000 tonnes of jute, sisal, and hemp into string, it would be 6.5 million km (4 million miles) long. It would stretch 17 times from the Earth to the Moon.

Timber
Worldwide, enough timber is cut every day to produce 150 million planks of wood. If all the logs cut in a day were used to build a tower, it would reach up into outer space.

"This pile of timber was built in one day, and it reaches right up into space – or so they tell me!"

"I'll sleep like a log after building this tower!"

"This is the cleanest ski slope I've ever seen!"

WASTE AND RECYCLING

RECYCLING RUBBISH MEANS that we take fewer raw materials from the Earth. Recycling paper the world over saves cutting down 5 million trees every day. Recycling also helps to save energy. The amount of energy needed to make one aluminium can from raw materials will make 20 cans from recycled aluminium. Most household waste can be recycled. Kitchen scraps can be composted, and glass taken to a bottle bank to be crushed and melted down to make new glass. Plastics can be shredded, melted, and reformed.

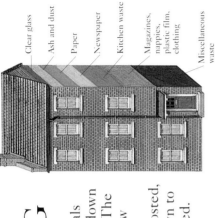

Clear glass

Ash and dust

Paper

Newspaper

Kitchen waste

Magazines, nappies, plastic film, clothing

Miscellaneous waste

Wasteful house

In one day, the average British household generates 1.74 kg (4 lb) of rubbish bin waste. In a year, this grows to the equivalent of the weight of 11 adults.

Nappy mountain

Babies in the USA get through 7,500 tonnes of disposable nappies every day. A day's worth of soiled nappies would fill 100,000 dustbins. Piled up, they would make a mountain as big as a 10-storey building.

Deforestation

Every day, enough tropical rainforest is cut down to cover an island as big as Barbados. During the 1980s, an area of forest was cut down that would have completely covered Germany.

One 12-m (40-ft) tree will make a stack of newspapers 1.2 m (4 ft) high.

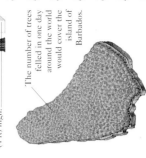

The number of trees felled in one day around the world would cover the island of Barbados.

The USA uses enough water in one day for each of its citizens to take 64 baths

World rubbish

If everyone in the world produced garbage at the rate of the average American, the world rubbish dump would grow by 12 million tonnes a day – equivalent to the weight of a herd of 2.4 million elephants. Fortunately, the world's rubbish heap grows by a mere two million tonnes every day.

Japan

Switzerland

Hungary

Luxembourg

Norway

Denmark

Netherlands

Canada

Finland

United States

Loads of rubbish

The world's top ten rubbish producers range from the USA with 2 kg (4 lb) of waste per person per day, to Japan, with 1 kg (2 lb).

Piles of waste

The large illustration shows waste and recycling figures for paper, cars, newspaper, kitchen appliances, tyres, cans, and clothes. The USA and Japan lag behind Germany, which has strict laws about recycling. It recycles around 20,000 tonnes of packaging materials in one day.

Paper in the USA

In one day, the USA throws away 202,000 tonnes of paper, of which 70,000 tonnes is recycled.

Paper in Japan

Japan uses 70,000 tonnes of paper in one day, and recycles more than half of it.

Cars

In the USA, 32,000 tonnes of cars are put on the scrap heap every day. 24,000 tonnes of materials from them are recycled.

Newspapers

28,000 tonnes of newsprint is dumped every day in the USA, of which 13,000 tonnes is recycled. Each Sunday edition of the *New York Times* produces 3,600 tonnes of waste.

USA and Japan

Every day in the USA, 520,000 tonnes of rubbish is produced. A fifth of that rubbish – 104,000 tonnes – is recycled. In Japan, 109,000 tonnes of rubbish is produced in one day. Japan recycles almost half its rubbish – 44,000 tonnes every day. Yet both countries are still very wasteful. Japan dumps 82,000 disposable plastic cameras every day. In the USA, 19,000 cu m (685,000 cu ft) of loose plastic "peanuts" are used in packaging every day – that's enough to fill 43 American homes or the passenger compartments of 22 jumbo jets.

United States

Composted 18,500 tonnes

Incinerated 81,000 tonnes

Recycled 104,000 tonnes

Landfill 316,500 tonnes

Japan

Composted 1,000 tonnes

Landfill 20,000 tonnes

Incinerated 44,000 tonnes

Recycled 44,000 tonnes

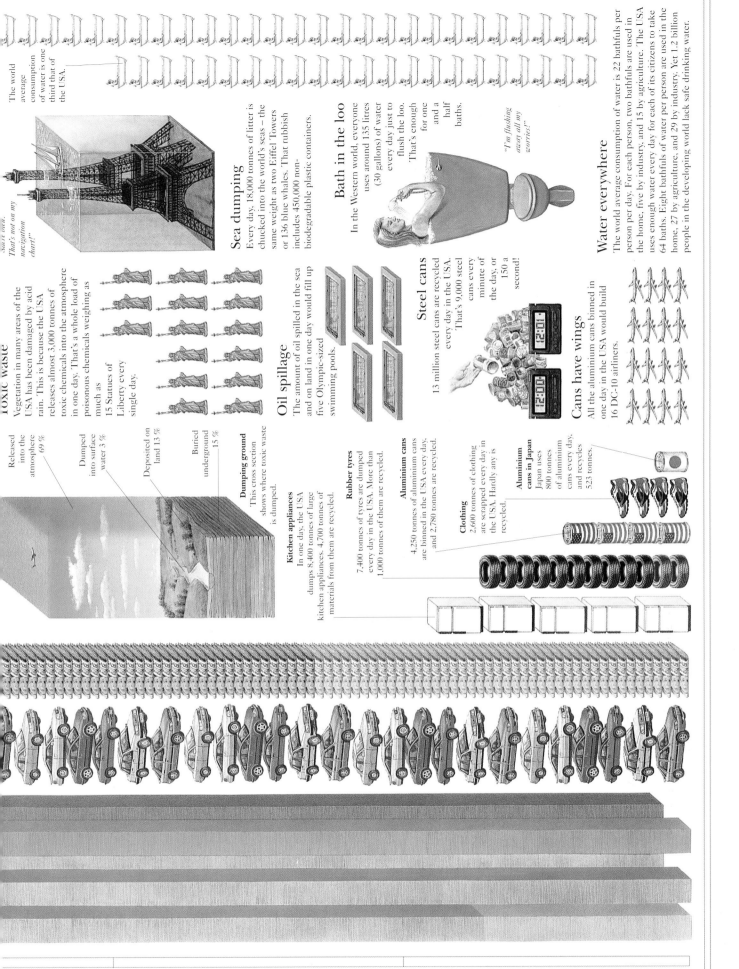

The world average consumption of water is one third that of the USA.

Sea dumping

Every day, 18,000 tonnes of litter is chucked into the world's seas – the same weight as two Eiffel Towers or 136 blue whales. That rubbish includes 450,000 non-biodegradable plastic containers.

"Sail oات. That's not on my navigation chart!"

Bath in the loo

In the Western world, everyone uses around 135 litres (30 gallons) of water every day just to flush the loo. That's enough for one and a half baths.

"I'm flushing away all my worries!"

Water everywhere

The world average consumption of water is 22 bathfuls per person per day. For each person, two bathfuls are used in the home, five by industry, and 15 by agriculture. The USA uses enough water every day for each of its citizens to take 64 baths. Eight bathfuls of water per person are used in the home, 27 by agriculture, and 29 by industry. Yet 1.2 billion people in the developing world lack safe drinking water.

TOXIC waste

Vegetation in many areas of the USA has been damaged by acid rain. This is because the USA releases almost 3,000 tonnes of toxic chemicals into the atmosphere in one day. That's a whole load of poisonous chemicals weighing as much as 15 Statues of Liberty every single day.

Released into the atmosphere 69 %

Dumped into surface water 3 %

Deposited on land 13 %

Buried underground 15 %

Dumping ground
This cross section shows where toxic waste is dumped.

Oil spillage

The amount of oil spilled in the sea and on land in one day would fill up five Olympic-sized swimming pools.

Steel cans

13 million steel cans are recycled every day in the USA. That's 9,000 steel cans every minute of the day, or 150 a second!

Cans have wings

All the aluminium cans binned in one day in the USA would build 16 DC-10 airliners.

Kitchen appliances
In one day, the USA dumps 8,400 tonnes of large kitchen appliances. 4,700 tonnes of materials from them are recycled.

Rubber tyres
7,400 tonnes of tyres are dumped every day in the USA. More than 1,000 tonnes of them are recycled.

Aluminium cans
4,250 tonnes of aluminium cans are binned in the USA every day, and 2,780 tonnes are recycled.

Clothing
2,600 tonnes of clothing are scrapped every day in the USA. Hardly any is recycled.

Aluminium cans in Japan
Japan uses 800 tonnes of aluminium cans every day, and recycles 523 tonnes.

COMMUNICATIONS

WORDS WERE FIRST SPOKEN BY HUMAN MOUTHS into human ears around 40,000 years ago. Today, words can reach destinations on the other side of the globe almost as soon as they are uttered. Radio signals are bounced back to receiving stations by the Earth's atmosphere, and satellites in space allow people to talk to each other, face to face, day and night, right across the planet. Our voices have escaped into space in the form of radio waves, and our first words have travelled more than 100 light years from the Earth. We have also beamed out messages, hoping to get in touch with alien beings – but as yet, no signal has been received from other worlds.

How satellite communications work

High-frequency signals for telephone, computer, and television pass straight through Earth's atmosphere. They need satellites in space to bounce them back to Earth. The higher the satellite, the greater the area of Earth it can cover

UOSAT 12
Each day, University of Surrey Satellite 12 travels 16 times around the Earth. It is testing a propulsion system that uses steam instead of poisonous gas.

OPTUS B
Optus B travels 864,000 (540,000 miles) each day, providing Australia and the Pacific with telephone and broadcasting links.

Meteosat weather satellite

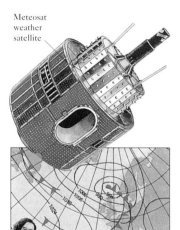

Meteosat

This Meteosat craft hovers over the Atlantic Ocean, from where it can "see" Europe's weather coming. Every day, it observes cloud movement, so weather forecasters can predict the weather for several days ahead.

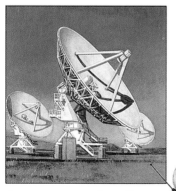

Is anyone out there?

Radio telescopes on Earth are listening day and night for messages from space, but after almost 40 years, not one has been picked up! In 1974 we sent a message to a distant star cluster from Arecibo Observatory, Puerto Rico, the world's biggest radio telescope. It will be the 270th century before it gets there, and the 520th century before we could receive a reply!

Defense Support Program
DSP is a US missile-warning satellite. Its infrared sensors can detect hot exhaust from a nuclear missile. It photographs some part of the Earth's surface six times every minute, which comes to 8,640 photographs a day.

SOHO
Every day, SOHO (Solar and Heliospheric Observatory) measures millions of sunquakes or vibrations on the surface of the Sun.

Iridium
This is one of a series of 66 low-Earth orbit communications satellites launched in 1997. Each day, Iridium can transfer thousands of calls from mobile phones.

Infrared Space Observatory
Each day, the tank of supercold helium in ISO cools instruments to −271° C, and allows them to measure tiny amounts of heat arriving from planets, gas clouds, and galaxies.

Molniya
Molniya provides communications coverage (television and telephone calls) for the most northerly regions of Russia for about eight hours every day.

Space Shuttle
In one day, the Space Shuttle can carry a crew of seven astronauts around the world 16 times, while they service and repair other craft, carry out scientific experiments, or take hundreds of photos of Earth.

"Sorry, wrong galaxy!"

Pioneer 10

The space probe Pioneer 10 was the first spacecraft to cross the asteroid belt and fly past Jupiter. It is now 15.6 billion km (9.7 billion miles) from Earth. Every day it travels 536,000 km (334,000 miles) into space.

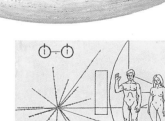

Message to other worlds

On its side, Pioneer 10 carries a plaque showing human figures and a diagram of the Earth's position in the Universe. It is hoped that one day aliens will find the craft and communicate with Earth.

Letters from America

The world sends 1.2 billion letters through the post every day. If all these letters could be stacked together, they would make a bridge that would span the Atlantic Ocean.

SA
The USA handles 20 million items of mail in one day.

UK
The UK handles around 52 million items of mail a day – that's one letter every day for each of the inhabitants of the British Isles.

SMALL WORLD

The Pentagon, Arlington, Virginia, is the headquarters of the American Department of Defense. It has one of the world's largest private telephone systems, with 34,500 individual lines, handling a million calls a day. It also has the world's largest pneumatic tube system, with 24 km (15 miles) of tube, through which letters are transported by means of air pressure.

HALCA
This Japanese radio astronomy satellite travels around Earth four times every day.

With love from me to you

Christmas Day is celebrated in the USA with 2.7 billion festive cards. One million romantic Americans lick stamps to catch the post for Valentine's Day on 14 February.

INTELSAT 8
Each day, Intelsats are able to relay up to 112,500 two-way telephone conversations at the same time, as well as three television channels.

Stampede

Americans stick around 13.7 million stamps every day. Pasted edge to edge, they would cover two American football fields.

"Any more glue and I'll get lockjaw!"

"I'm out of the country right now."

'Allo? 'Allo?

Every day, 730 million telephone lines and more than 200 million mobile phones are in use across the world. Most of the talking goes on in North America. The average American makes five calls a day. If the total daily calls between the USA and Canada were added up into a single conversation, they would make a telephone call 23 years long!

"Your Shuttle needs servicing, mate."

NAVSTAR
NAVSTAR is a series of 24 navigation satellites. Each satellite travels around the Earth twice a day, sending signals that help boats and planes to locate their positions.

ACTS
The Advanced Communications Technology Satellite takes exactly 24 hours to orbit the Earth as it spins on its axis.

"Salut!"
"Bore da!"
"Hello!"
"Jambo!"
"Iska warran!"
"Hej!"
"Ciao!"

Lots of chat

Every day, people around the world communicate with each other in thousands of different languages, each with its own culture and traditions.

Hubble Space Telescope
Each day, HST takes pictures of planets, stars, dust clouds, black holes, and quasars. With new cameras fitted in 1997, HST can see far back into the past, detecting the first galaxies soon after they were born.

Computer-speak

Computers were first used for communications in 1969 by scientists and academics. Now, over 160 million users around the globe talk to each other every day on the Internet.

"Dumela!"
"Hoi!"
"Alo!"
"Kumusta!"
"Bloomin' bootiful!"

Don't shoot the messenger

Every business day, Federal Express delivers more than two million items to over 200 countries around the world.

Flower power

Every day, the British communicate happiness, sympathy, or regret by sending 11,000 bunches of flowers.

A DAY TO REMEMBER

Dots and dashes

On 8 January 1838, the first Morse Code message was sent by a student of Samuel Morse. It read: "A patient waiter is no loser."

Altitude problem

The biro was patented on 10 June 1943 by László Josef Biró. It was used by navigators, as fountain pens leak at altitude, and pencils do not mark weatherproof maps.

Royal cable

On 16 August 1858, Queen Victoria sent a formal greeting to American President James Buchanan. She was the first head of state to use the world's first transatlantic cable.

TRAVEL

IF ALL THE FOOTSTEPS TAKEN IN THE WORLD in one day could be put together to make one long journey, the human race could walk 88 times to the Sun and back every 24 hours. On wheels, wings, water, and on its feet, this restless world is constantly on the move. Travelling is more comfortable for some than for others. In the West, there is a car for every two people. In Ethiopia, there is only one car for every 1,468 people.

World flights

Every day there are 45,000 scheduled flights carrying more than 3.5 million passengers. This is equivalent to the total population of Puerto Rico taking to the skies.

On the go all day

How far could the different forms of transport in this fleet travel in a day if each one maintained its maximum cruising speed over 24 hours? In reality, of course, fuel tanks would run dry, engines would overheat, and stamina would flag long before the day was out.

Passenger helicopter
Cruises at 241 kph (150 mph). In 24 hours, it could travel 5,784 km (3,600 miles).

Concorde
Cruises at 2,222 kph (1,450 mph). In 24 hours, it could cover 53,328 km (34,800 miles).

Boeing 747-400
Cruises at 901 kph (560 mph). In 24 hours, it could travel 21,624 km (13,440 miles).

SeaCat ferry
Cruises at 64 kph (40 mph). In 24 hours, it could cover 1,536 km (960 miles).

Gas balloon
Travels at 16 kph (10 mph). In 24 hours, it could cover 384 km (240 miles).

Hovercraft
Travels at 120 kph (75 mph). In 24 hours, it could cover 2,880 km (1,800 miles).

Japanese Series E2 train
Cruises at 275 kph (171 mph). In 24 hours, it could cover 6,600 km (4,104 miles).

Motorbike
Can cruise at 129 kmh (80 mph). In 24 hours it could cover 3,096 km (1,920 miles).

Heathrow Airport

London Heathrow has more international passengers than any other airport in the world. On an average day, it handles 105,000 passengers, 2,000 tonnes of freight – which might include racing cars and racehorses, as well as exotic fruit and vegetables – and 200 tonnes of mail. Every day, 1,200 aircraft land and take off. The airport's busiest day so far was 30 June 1995, when 194,500 passengers passed through it.

European coach and personnel carrier
Both these vehicles can cruise along the motorway at 113 kph (70 mph). In 24 hours they would cover 2,712 km (1,680 miles).

Personnel carrier

Every day, 35,000 of Heathrow's passengers travel on to a further destination.

93 different airlines operate at Heathrow.

Each aircraft holds an average of 130 passengers.

Every day, Heathrow has 36 flights to Paris and 22 flights to New York.

156,000 items of baggage pass through Heathrow Airport every day.

Every day, 40–50 Very Important Persons get special treatment as they pass through the airport.

Heathrow's cafés and bars sell 26,000 cups of tea and coffee, 6,500 pints of beer and 6,500 sandwiches every day.

BRITISH AIRWAYS

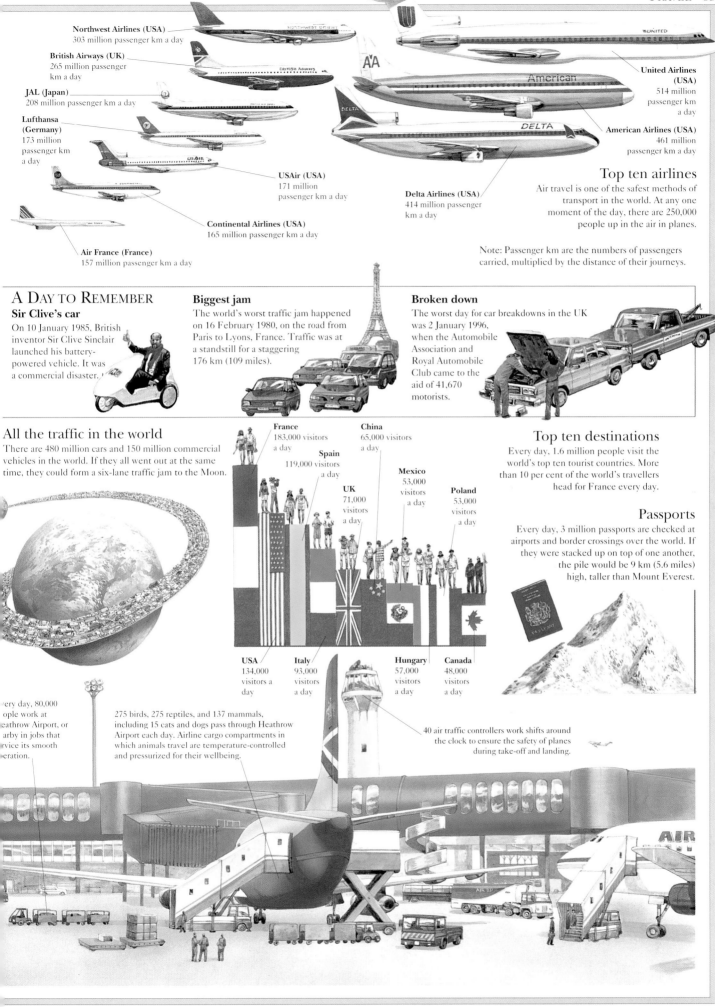

Northwest Airlines (USA)
303 million passenger km a day

British Airways (UK)
265 million passenger
km a day

JAL (Japan)
208 million passenger km a day

Lufthansa
(Germany)
173 million
passenger km
a day

USAir (USA)
171 million
passenger km a day

Continental Airlines (USA)
165 million passenger km a day

Air France (France)
157 million passenger km a day

United Airlines
(USA)
514 million
passenger km
a day

American Airlines (USA)
461 million
passenger km a day

Delta Airlines (USA)
414 million passenger
km a day

Top ten airlines

Air travel is one of the safest methods of
transport in the world. At any one
moment of the day, there are 250,000
people up in the air in planes.

Note: Passenger km are the numbers of passengers
carried, multiplied by the distance of their journeys.

A DAY TO REMEMBER

Sir Clive's car

On 10 January 1985, British
inventor Sir Clive Sinclair
launched his battery-
powered vehicle. It was
a commercial disaster.

Biggest jam

The world's worst traffic jam happened
on 16 February 1980, on the road from
Paris to Lyons, France. Traffic was at
a standstill for a staggering
176 km (109 miles).

Broken down

The worst day for car breakdowns in the UK
was 2 January 1996,
when the Automobile
Association and
Royal Automobile
Club came to the
aid of 41,670
motorists.

All the traffic in the world

There are 480 million cars and 150 million commercial
vehicles in the world. If they all went out at the same
time, they could form a six-lane traffic jam to the Moon.

France
183,000 visitors
a day

Spain
119,000 visitors
a day

China
65,000 visitors
a day

UK
71,000
visitors
a day

Mexico
53,000
visitors
a day

Poland
53,000
visitors
a day

USA
134,000
visitors a
day

Italy
93,000
visitors
a day

Hungary
57,000
visitors
a day

Canada
48,000
visitors
a day

Top ten destinations

Every day, 1.6 million people visit the
world's top ten tourist countries. More
than 10 per cent of the world's travellers
head for France every day.

Passports

Every day, 3 million passports are checked at
airports and border crossings over the world. If
they were stacked up on top of one another,
the pile would be 9 km (5.6 miles)
high, taller than Mount Everest.

Every day, 80,000
people work at
Heathrow Airport, or
nearby in jobs that
service its smooth
operation.

275 birds, 275 reptiles, and 137 mammals,
including 15 cats and dogs pass through Heathrow
Airport each day. Airline cargo compartments in
which animals travel are temperature-controlled
and pressurized for their wellbeing.

40 air traffic controllers work shifts around
the clock to ensure the safety of planes
during take-off and landing.

A DAY OFF

WHAT DO YOU DO when you have time to yourself? Do you spring into action and ride off on your bike, or put on your in-line skates? Or do you do as little as possible and simply sit down in front of the TV, or sin in the bath? Do you want to be thrilled and entertain at a theme park or at the cinema? Do you travel the world and marvel at its wonders, from the mighty Grand Canyon to the Great Pyramid? Whatever you do, you will be surprised to discover how many other people are spending the day doing it too!

The Grand Canyon, Arizona, USA, has 12,000 visitors a day.

The CN Tower, Toronto, Canada, attracts 5,000 visitors a day.

Kennedy Space Center, Florida, USA, sells 1,500 tickets to admit visitors to watch the launch of the Shuttle.

The Empire State Building, New York, USA, attracts 7,000 visitors a day.

The Blackpool Tower, Blackpool, UK, draws 3,300 visitors a day.

Uluru, Northern Territory, Australia, has 900 visitors a day.

Stonehenge, Wiltshire, UK, attracts 2,200 visitors a day.

Kew Gardens, London, UK, has 2,700 visitors a day.

The Tower of London, London, UK, attracts 7,600 visitors a day.

The Eiffel Tower, Paris, France, attracts 15,000 visitors a day.

The Great Pyramid, Giza, Egypt, draws 10,000 visitors a day.

Old Faithful Geyser, Yellowstone National Park, USA, has 8,000 visitors a day.

A day out, a night out

All the world loves a day out. Every day, 173,000 people visit America's National Parks. The world's most spectacular night out is offered by Monte Carlo. Every night for a week in July and August each year, as part of an international competition, one tonne of fireworks are launched into the skies above the Mediterranean harbour.

French camping

The French have a passion for camping, and an abundance of beautiful countryside in which to pitch their tents. Every night, nearly 3 million French people sleep under canvas.

Bombay

"Stop crackling that popadom, I can't hear the film!"

Indian movies

India is the most film-loving nation in the world. It has 13,000 screens, including 4,000 mobile cinemas. Every day, 15 million Indians visit the movies That's like having the whole populatio of Bombay, India's film-making capital at the cinema.

Universal Studios, California, USA, draws 14,000 visitors a day.

The British Museu London, UK, has 15,400 visitors a da

The Louvre Museum, Paris, France, attracts 17,000 visitors every day.

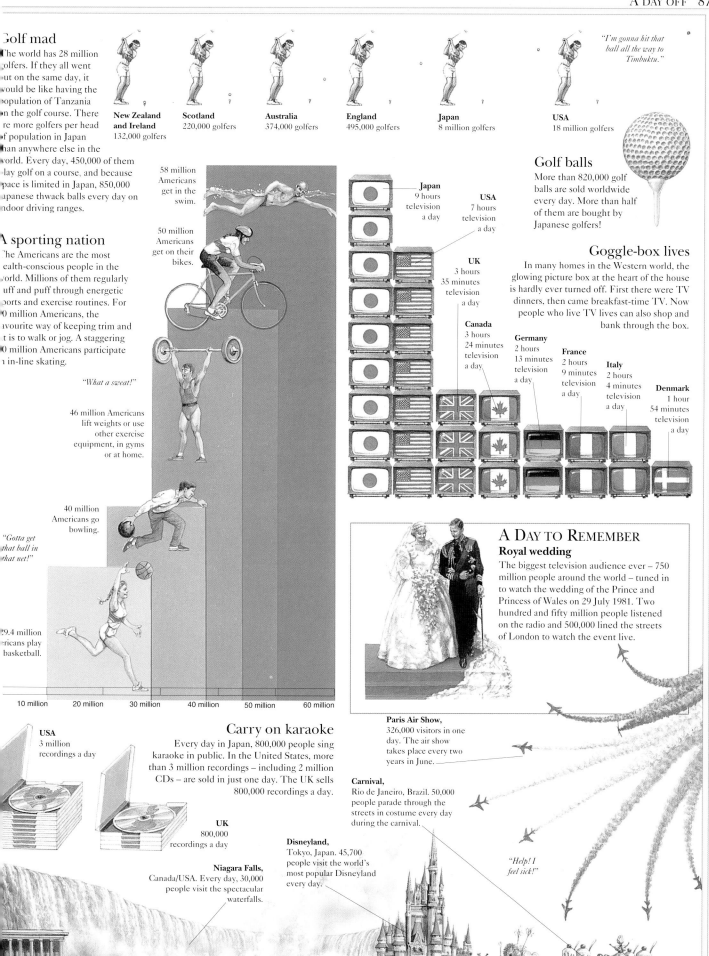

Golf mad

The world has 28 million golfers. If they all went out on the same day, it would be like having the population of Tanzania on the golf course. There are more golfers per head of population in Japan than anywhere else in the world. Every day, 450,000 of them play golf on a course, and because space is limited in Japan, 850,000 Japanese thwack balls every day on indoor driving ranges.

New Zealand and Ireland
132,000 golfers

Scotland
220,000 golfers

Australia
374,000 golfers

England
495,000 golfers

Japan
8 million golfers

USA
18 million golfers

"I'm gonna hit that ball all the way to Timbuktu."

Golf balls

More than 820,000 golf balls are sold worldwide every day. More than half of them are bought by Japanese golfers!

A sporting nation

The Americans are the most health-conscious people in the world. Millions of them regularly huff and puff through energetic sports and exercise routines. For [...]0 million Americans, the favourite way of keeping trim and [fi]t is to walk or jog. A staggering [...]0 million Americans participate in in-line skating.

58 million Americans get in the swim.

50 million Americans get on their bikes.

"What a sweat!"

46 million Americans lift weights or use other exercise equipment, in gyms or at home.

40 million Americans go bowling.

"Gotta get that ball in that net!"

[2]9.4 million [Am]ericans play basketball.

10 million   20 million   30 million   40 million   50 million   60 million

Goggle-box lives

In many homes in the Western world, the glowing picture box at the heart of the house is hardly ever turned off. First there were TV dinners, then came breakfast-time TV. Now people who live TV lives can also shop and bank through the box.

Japan
9 hours television a day

USA
7 hours television a day

UK
3 hours 35 minutes television a day

Canada
3 hours 24 minutes television a day

Germany
2 hours 13 minutes television a day

France
2 hours 9 minutes television a day

Italy
2 hours 4 minutes television a day

Denmark
1 hour 54 minutes television a day

A DAY TO REMEMBER
Royal wedding

The biggest television audience ever – 750 million people around the world – tuned in to watch the wedding of the Prince and Princess of Wales on 29 July 1981. Two hundred and fifty million people listened on the radio and 500,000 lined the streets of London to watch the event live.

Carry on karaoke

Every day in Japan, 800,000 people sing karaoke in public. In the United States, more than 3 million recordings – including 2 million CDs – are sold in just one day. The UK sells 800,000 recordings a day.

USA
3 million recordings a day

UK
800,000 recordings a day

Paris Air Show,
326,000 visitors in one day. The air show takes place every two years in June.

Carnival,
Rio de Janeiro, Brazil. 50,000 people parade through the streets in costume every day during the carnival.

Disneyland,
Tokyo, Japan. 45,700 people visit the world's most popular Disneyland every day.

Niagara Falls,
Canada/USA. Every day, 30,000 people visit the spectacular waterfalls.

"Help! I feel sick!"

INDEX

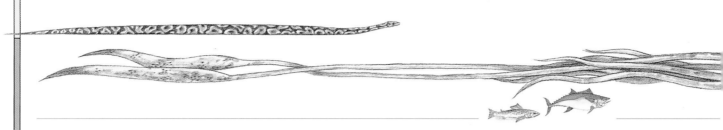

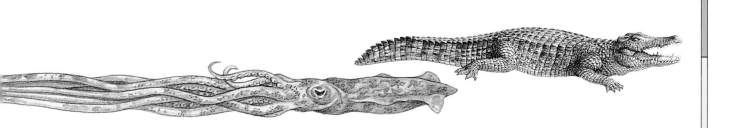

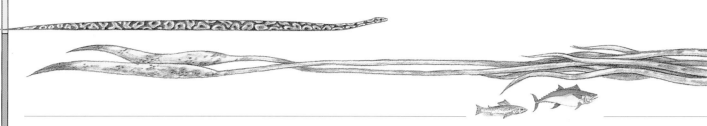

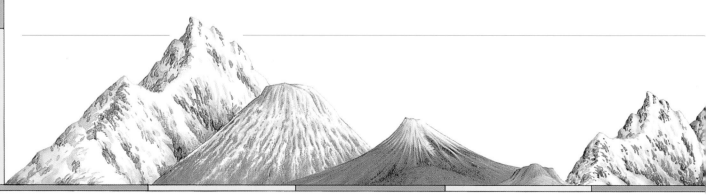

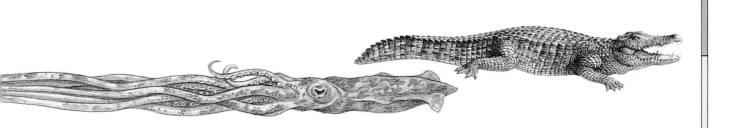

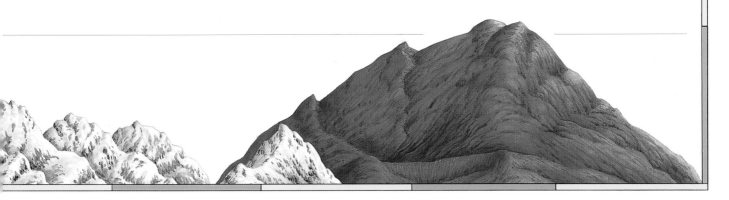

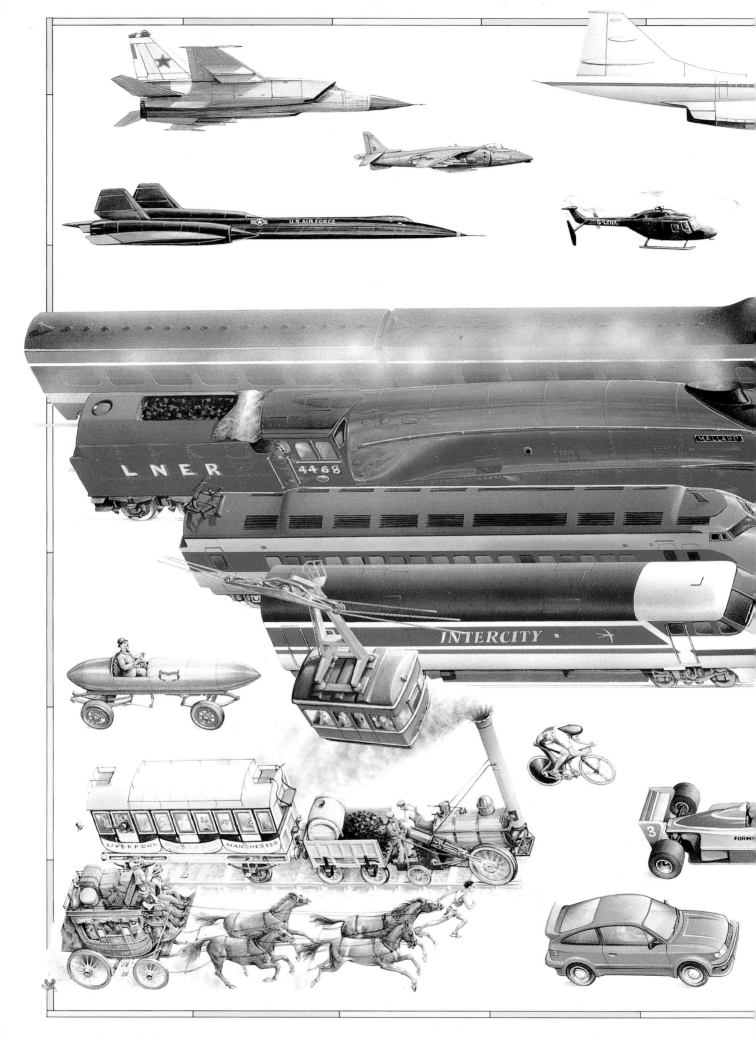

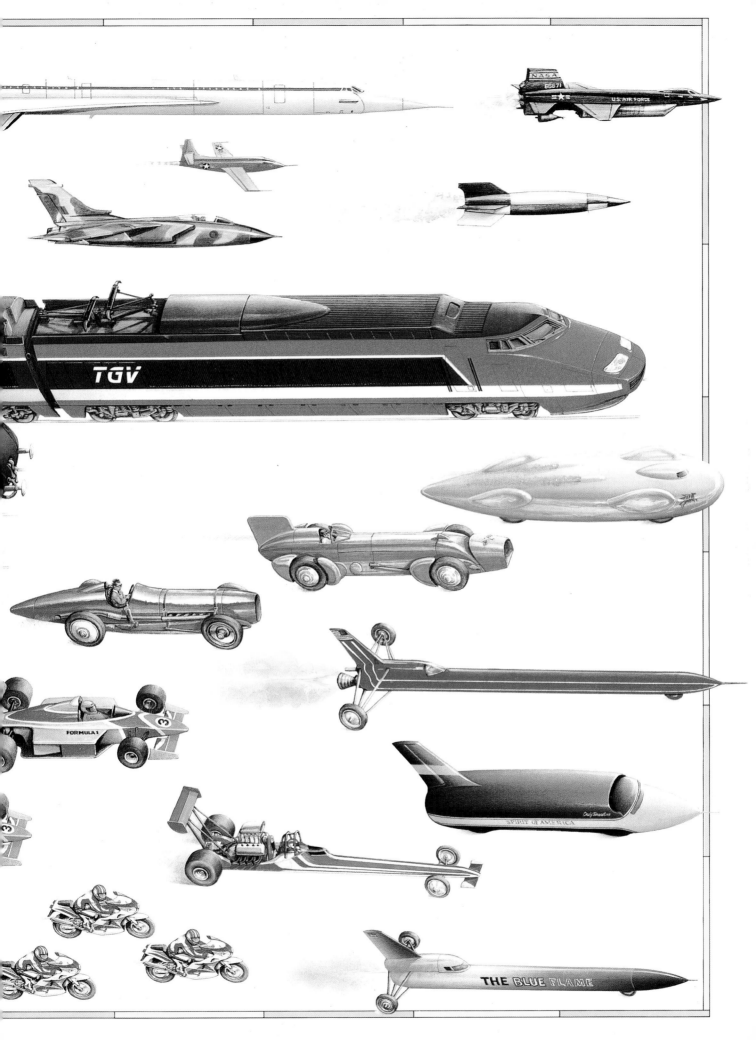

ACKNOWLEDGEMENTS

**Dorling Kindersley would like to thank
the following for helping with this book –**

Design: Jo Earl, Jim Miles, Sheilagh Noble, Simon Faires

Editorial: Terry Martin, Richard Platt, Phil Wilkinson, Francesca
Baines, Robert Graham, Angela Koo, Nichola Roberts

Index: Chris Bernstein

Illustrations: Russell Barnett, Michael Courtney, Angelika
Elsbach, Richard Bonson, Stephen Conlin, Peter Dennis (Linda
Rogers Associates), Chris Forsey, Malcolm Mcgregor, and Peter
Visscher

Research: Professor John Allen; Amateur Yacht Research
Society; Cameron Balloons; Carluccio's; Chicago Bridge & Iron
Company; Dr Peter Cotgreave, London Zoo; Edificio Petróleos
de Venezuela; Robert Graham; Hapag Lloyd; Kitty Hauser;
Esther Labi; Lindstrand Balloons; Lloyd's List; Keith Lye;
Natural History Museum; P & O; Steve Parker;
Royal Botanic Gardens, Kew;
Silja Shipping; World Sailing Records

Additional acknowledgements: The Automobile Association;
Biosphere II; Peter Bond; Gary Booth; Heathrow Airport; Keith
Lye; Milton Keynes Recycling Facility; Royal Automobile Club;
Royal Horticultural Society Library; Martin Walters; Richard
Walters; World Resources Foundation

Special thanks to Caroline Ash